WHY PEOPLE JOIN THE CHURCH

Why People Join the Church

An Exploratory Study

Edward A. Rauff

Lutheran Council in the U.S.A.

THE PILGRIM PRESS | GLENMARY RESEARCH

New York | *Washington, D.C.*

GRC A-63 / P-351
November, 1979

THE PILGRIM PRESS, 132 West 31 Street, New York, N.Y. 10001.
ISBN: 0-8298-0387-4. $5.95

GLENMARY RESEARCH CENTER, 4606 East-West Highway, Washington,
D.C. 20014. The Glenmary Research Center was established in 1966 to help serve
the research needs of the Catholic Church in rural America.

Contents

Preface

This is an exploratory study focusing not on statistics but rather on the voices of 180 ordinary men and women as they recall their spiritual journeys from outside to inside the doors of the Church. The stories are at times extraordinarily untidy and ambiguous, at other times simple and moving.

Many people I talked with indicated that this was the first time they had ever been asked about their "back to Church pilgrimage." The question had never before been raised. Once it had, they were moved to share thoughtful and sometimes profound insights into their own spiritual development and to talk about the shift in their lifestyles that joining the Church caused. I had the feeling that some said more than they had at first intended to say.

Because of the nature of this exploratory study, I have not attempted the type of sampling required for strictly scientific validity, but have merely brought together the taped comments of men and women who had been unchurched for several years and have recently joined the Church, and also more than 40 church leaders and pastors. The interviews were conducted during the last half of 1978, in eight diverse counties in the United States.

This study was made possible through the financial assistance of the members of the Aid Association for Lutherans, in Appleton, Wisconsin and the Glenmary Research Center, in Washington, D.C., and through the willingness of the Lutheran Council in the U.S.A. to approve my sabbatical plans. Special thanks to Fr. Bernard Quinn, of the Glenmary Research Center, who gave me guidance at various stages of the project, and to Dr. David Byers, who edited the manuscript. Dr. Russell Hale of the Lutheran Seminary in Gettysburg, author of *Who Are the Unchurched?*, stimulated my interest and encouraged me to ask further questions. In my absence from the Lutheran Council, my ground support included Alice Kendrick and Dale Farley, who kept my office humming. Naomi Frost gave invaluable editorial assistance and Dan Sendzik typed the recorded interviews. My wife, Elaine, and my children also deserve thanks for keeping things on an even keel, and so freeing me for travel and writing.

The main credit, however, goes to those persons who shared with me the story of how God and the Church have moved in their lives. May their words encourage those within the Church to see with new eyes what the Church means, and those outside to consider giving the Church a chance.

1

Introduction

To say, "Let's go to church," is deceptively simple. What picture does the phrase conjure up? A family rushing out the front door on Sunday morning? People entering the church doors, greeting one another warmly? When Gallup Poll interviewers asked a sampling of Americans, "Did you happen to attend church or synagogue in the last seven days, or not?" 40 percent answered "Yes." Translated into numbers, that indicates that about 85 million Americans on a given workship day responded positively to the invitation "Let's go to church."

But the answer is not automatic for a majority of Americans. For singles, living far from family and friends, for workers on long shifts who agree heartily that the Sabbath is a day of rest, for those who have exhausted all the resources for entertainment on a frantic Saturday night—it may not be so easy to go to church. For the millions that are uprooted to begin life in a new community without the support systems that gave them strong encouragement in their former parish, "church" means a strange building with an unfamiliar pastor and members whose friendliness is questionable

at best. For the young to submit themselves to an adult-run institution that aims its rules and regulations at them and uses cultural
forms, like art and music, galactically far from their own, seems
almost a denial of identity. Many have dropped out and joined the
ranks of the unchurched.

There has been a new interest in the unchurched in the 1970's.
An ambitious study done by the Gallup organization in 1978 was
funded by a large number of church agencies and denominations.
The report, *The Unchurched American*,[1] which resulted from this
study, indicated that most of America's unchurched did not consider themselves unbelievers or non-religious. Few "cracker-
barrel atheists" or searching agnostics were unearthed. The great
majority simply "fell out" of affiliation with a church.

Through the lush years of church growth, cresting in the 1960's,
so many new church members commanded attention that the existence of the unchurched appeared insignificant. In fact, it seemed
that those who were outside the ecclesial doors were really potential members just waiting to be invited. As a young Lutheran
pastor in Columbus, Ohio in the late 1950's, I was boasting to a
neighbor who was pastor of a Presbyterian church about the
rapid growth of our little congregation. He looked at me coolly
and said, with more condescension than criticism in his voice,
"You'd have to be absolutely obnoxious not to succeed in the
Church today."

Migrants to suburban developments found little that offered
social life there except the churches. And they joined in large
numbers. All the mainline denominations reported remarkable
growth. But as this surge began to slow down, flatten out and
finally decline, some began to ask, "Why?"

A small consortium of church agency people, soon after the
1970 census, formed CAPC (Census Access for Planning in the
Church). These staff people, mostly research directors for the denominations, committed themselves to analyzing the communities

---

1. *The Unchurched American 1978*. A Study Conducted for the Religious Coali-
tion to Study Backgrounds, Values and Interests of Unchurched Americans, by
the Princeton Religion Research Center and the Gallup Organization, Inc., n.d.

in which churches were growing or declining or standing still. What made the difference? What factors in a community would foster and nurture a mission congregation of a certain denomination?

In a somewhat related move, another group organized to conduct a religious census, by church body, of all 3,156 counties in the United States, their work culminating in the publication of *Churches and Church Membership in the United States: 1971.*[2] Included in the volume is a map showing the major denomination of each county. Not only did each county show the denomination's strength, but whole regional pictures began to emerge that graphically illustrated the sweep of American church history.

Comparing the census and the church membership data, the Glenmary Research Center also published a map entitled *Percent of Population Unchurched.* Subtracting all the reported church members in a county from the county population left a number representing the unchurched, people not counted on the rolls of any of the denominations that participated in the church membership study. It became apparent from this map that the unchurched were found more commonly in some regions than others. The factors explaining this were as yet unclear.

Professor J. Russell Hale of the Lutheran Theological Seminary in Gettysburg chose six diverse counties, widely separated from one another, for further study. One characteristic common to all the counties was that more than 50 percent of the population in each was unchurched. This was well above the national average of 38 percent unchurched. Each of the six counties was in a larger region where neighboring counties also showed a high proportion of unchurched people. Interviewing people with no church affiliation in these counties, Hale tried to find an answer to the question, "Why do some regions in the country score higher in the un-

2. Douglas W. Johnson, Paul R. Picard and Bernard Quinn, *Churches and Church Membership in the United States: An Enumeration by Region, State and County 1971.* A study sponsored jointly by the Office of Research, Evaluation and Planning of the National Council of the Churches of Christ in the U.S.A., the Department of Research and Statistics of the Lutheran Church—Missouri Synod, and the Glenmary Research Center. (Washington, D.C.: Glenmary Research Center, 1974).

churched column than others?" Publishing his findings in a fascinating report entitled *Who Are the Unchurched?*[3] Hale presented anecdotal material from more than 160 interviews, giving face and voice and conviction to representatives of America's 80 million unchurched. He also tried to explain why some regions in our country were especially fertile ground for the unchurched—or, to look at it from a different perspective, were inhospitable fields for the churched.

Following in his steps two years later, I traveled in turn to the same six counties: Polk County, Oregon; Orange County, California; Waldo County, Maine; Boone County, West Virginia; Marion County, Alabama; and Sarasota County, Florida. I added a seventh county, Ingham in southern Michigan, to include another metropolitan area and also to tap the populous Great Lakes states. Ten interviews were carried out in New York City as "practice." But the resulting narratives were too unusual to shelve. I have included some quotes from them. My quest was somewhat different from Russell Hale's. Hale cast his net out to the unchurched of America—or at least to those dwelling in the six counties. I sought the opposite side of the coin. The questions that interested me were, "Are there people in counties with a majority of their population unchurched who have swum against the stream, who without community pressure or support have joined a Church? Why did people who were unchurched make an about-face? What is their story?"

A more important question soon appeared, "What clues can these people give to the pastors and church leaders about how religious needs can be met and how a spiritual journey can be guided to a church home?" Considering some of the reasons people gave for joining a church, a congregation could ask itself, "Does our church attract or repel such seekers? What shifts in emphasis in our church programming might extend our welcoming hand farther? Why should such people consider joining our church?"

3. J. Russell Hale, *Who Are the Unchurched? An Exploratory Study* (Washington, D.C.: Glenmary Research Center, 1977).

These questions define the place I have carved out. It is a space next to but separate from Hale's pioneering work. Inevitably there will be some similarities—I traveled many of the same roads in those counties, patronized the local motels and restaurants, worshiped in some of the same churches and perhaps even talked with the same people. In two cases I even interviewed people whom Hale had contacted two years earlier. One family in Maine was unchurched two years ago and has since joined a Methodist congregation. And a young woman in Alabama also changed her status; she's now a new Catholic.

For an astute analysis of the factors active in each county which seem to foster an unchurched lifestyle, I refer the reader to *Who Are the Unchurched?* In it Hale examines the historical roots of the communities and analyzes what is going on, underlining the dominant trends in each county. Rather than re-examine those factors, this report concentrates on new data.

PROCESS

An initial letter went out in spring 1978 to most of the churches in each county. After describing the purpose of my study, I asked the clergy to consider if there were formerly unchurched people now in their congregations who met these criteria:

- 18 years of age and older;
- unchurched for at least five years;
- joined the church within the last ten years;
- currently active members;
- would be willing to tell their story in a confidential interview.

Upon arrival in the county I would usually make contact with the clergy, most conveniently at a breakfast, and both set out my goals and ask for their suggestions. Then I would solicit names, telephone those selected for appointments, and begin interviewing people of different denominations and ethnic groups, hopefully in proportion to their total numbers in the county. This was not always possible. Some congregations had received no new members, while one or two others, with active evangelism programs or outstanding clergy, could offer me many names—sometimes more than I could use. One extroverted preacher assured me he could give me "a hundred names"; I settled for six. In only a few instances were the clergy uncooperative. One said he didn't want his people "probed." Asked, "Do you have any members of your parish who were formerly unchurched?" more than one pastor of a large congregation answered, "How am I supposed to know?" I made some suggestions, but some still could not be bothered.

In a few cases I ran into some residual resentment to Hale's study of the unchurched two years prior to my arrival. Apparently some newspaper articles had leaned on the more sensational aspects of the research instead of trying to give a balanced picture. In Sarasota, for example, a Baptist minister, whom I had phoned for an appointment, met me in the parking lot. He didn't want to let me loose in his congregation, gathered for midweek supper, before he had checked me out. He was still smarting from the publicity which had emphasized the unchurched character of the county and implied the failure of the churches to meet their challenge. One dignitary elsewhere, upon receiving some advance notice of my project, protested in a television editorial, "We think spiritual values in _____ County have been erroneously misjudged."

Membership

How do we define churched and unchurched? That question confronted me early in my research. "Membership" is a term that does not have a universally agreed upon definition. This was evident in some of the difficulties I encountered when I asked pastors for the names of people who were unchurched but who now have joined a church.

For some *Catholic* pastors the concept of unchurched had to be amplified. A Catholic who has been baptized in the Church is considered a member, even though he or she might not have attended church for several years. The membership is not in doubt. That person is considered a Catholic and will remain so in the eyes of the Church. Baptism is the authentic entrance and the indelible incorporation into the Church. So I had to redefine unchurched,

for my own research purposes, to include those who were still considered members but who were functionally outside of the Church's
sacramental ministry. That is, Catholics who had not attended
Mass for five or more years, I considered unchurched. And those
who had renewed their affiliation with the worshiping fellowship,
after such a hiatus, would fit under the term "previously unchurched."

The terms "confirmed members" and "communicant members"
were not very meaningful in a Catholic context. In fact, a reader
of *Churches and Church Membership 1971* can observe that the
Catholic population is shown only under the heading of "total adherents." Under the heading "confirmed or communicant membership," the figure next to the Catholic listing is always zero! There
is no concept of membership other than baptized members. So the
term "convert" also had to be redefined for my purposes. Since I
wanted to interview people previously unchurched, those who
had been active in a different denomination before they became
Catholics had to be excluded. Of course I was interested in those
who had been raised in another fellowship but had fallen out of
the practice of that Faith for at least five years before converting.

To become a member of the Catholic Church, one is baptized
into that Faith, preferably at the earliest age. Adults or youth who
were baptized into another Christian Church can become Catholic
by profession of faith after instruction for somewhere between six
and twenty weeks in an "inquiry class." Unbaptized youth or
adults usually wait until completing the course of study to be
baptized.

A similar emphasis is true for the *Baptist* family of Churches,
including other denominations which practice "believers' Baptism." Baptism is offered to those people who have experienced
the reality of salvation and desire baptism in response to that
experience, believed to be the Spirit's activity making one "born
again." This experience is often precipitated by preaching aimed
at conversion, or by the congregation's regular invitation or "altar
call." At the time of invitation people are also prayed for and encouraged by hymns, testimonies and exhortations.

The emphasis in these Churches is not on being born into the Faith or being instructed in its doctrines. Rather it is on God's activity, moving one to faith, and on the individual's applying the Spirit's invitation to himself or herself and accepting it. So Baptism is again the valid entrance, but on different terms from that offered to infants. The absence of a spoken confession or an experience of being born again on the part of infants or small children would cause those of the "believers' Baptism" tradition to deny that Baptism in its biblical understanding has taken place for such children. Only a minority of Baptist Churches practice "open membership," which accepts members transferred from other Churches without rebaptism.

The mode of Baptism also differs, with immersion being the preferred form. The baptismal immersion site can be a pool in the sanctuary, a river, lake, swimming pool, or, in California and certain other charmed locations, a magnificently scenic cove of the ocean where perhaps hundreds or thousands gather for the rite. Unbaptized infants and small children who are associated by family with a congregation are not considered members until they are baptized. In *Churches and Church Membership 1971*, a mathematical formula was devised to include the number of children under thirteen so that these Churches would have a membership total comparable to others who count children because of their Baptism as infants.

Lutherans, *Episcopalians*, and certain others of a sacramental tradition have different categories of membership. They count baptized and confirmed members as two discrete categories. Practicing infant Baptism, and therefore careful to count all small children, they also confirm the baptized children when they reach the age of 10 to 18, with the majority being confirmed in the eighth or ninth grades. In the Episcopal Church, the bishop performs the confirmation rite with laying on of hands. Baptized membership includes confirmed members, but adds to that number those who are baptized though unconfirmed.

In many parishes Sunday School children are urged to receive Baptism. If they and their families agree, the children may become baptized members even though their families may still remain outside of the Church. There is a recent tendency in these Churches to be less generous in baptizing children from families which are not closely affiliated with the congregations, and therefore might be untrustworthy in carrying out the promises made on behalf of the children. But the idea of withholding baptism from little children is repugnant to many pastors.

For pastors of these Churches, the term "unchurched" would also include people who have spent years away from formal worship service, although they may still be on a membership roll. Congregations are ambivalent about dropping inactive members. Some set up forms for admonition of the inactive and may even follow prescribed steps and timetables which may cause the unresponsive to be excluded from the membership list. Other congregations, admitting the practical difficulties in dealing with the lapsed who are thus dropped, slip such names onto an "inactive" list, sometimes called a "responsibility" list. These lapsed members are not dismissed completely from the Church's oversight. Those who are intent on having the lapsed member say "yea" or "nay" claim that avoiding such confrontation allows the inactive person to rest in false security. Some Lutheran yearbooks also list categories of members in addition to baptized and confirmed. "Communicant" members are those who have received Holy Communion at least once during the year, and "active" members are those who have communed or contributed within the year.

In *Presbyterian, Reformed, United Church of Christ, Methodist,* and other related traditions, the confirmed or communicant designation is used to define persons who are counted as members of that denomination and congregation. Baptism is administered to infants and small children if desired, but only when one is confirmed in the Faith after appropriate instruction does one "become" a Presbyterian or full member of that denomination or another related church body. Inactive members may have their membership lifted in official conference action when a governing body notes their continual absence from worship, communion and stewardship. A way for re-entry into membership is offered under the rubric "reaffirmation of faith," usually in public profession.

Membership is claimed by people who have studied the teachings of the Church, accepted its claims, promised their loyalty and obedience to the Church's ministration, and expressed their desire to enter into covenantal relationship with God and the Church. For children of church families and other interested young people, training takes place usually in the junior high or high school years. Adult converts can join the Churches through instruction classes and a public profession of faith.

Evangelical Churches, including *Christian and Missionary Alliance, Assembly of God, Pentecostal, Nazarene, Church of God*, and various independent conservative Churches, have differing standards for membership. I was surprised to find that the membership roll of some congregations may be much smaller than the total number of people attending worship services on a Sunday. Membership is withheld until the seeker has indicated a willingness to accept all the responsibilities that members assume. These might include abstinence from tobacco and alcohol, commitment to faithful worship and prayer life, tithing, and acceptance of the authority of the congregation.

On the other hand, some of these Churches offer membership merely upon request. Said one southern California pastor, "You can't find out how to join this place by any encouragement or push or pull from the pulpit. Oh, we have an altar call, but that's to join Jesus Christ, not to join this Church. 'Cause if you've accepted Jesus Christ as your personal Lord and Savior, and you want your name on the membership rolls, you go in there and you say, 'How do I join?' They'll say, 'Well, you just found out. You asked.' " This pastor is apparently casual about membership, but many thousands of people attend his church each week. His explanation is, "They have to continue to come here because there's something here that they want." A minister in Sarasota, Florida said, "We have no membership. We believe if a person's a Christian, he's part of the general, universal Church of Christ, or Church of God, or whatever name you want to put on the Church." Large baptismal services are held by these Churches periodically. With no denominational structure to report to, independent congregations are indifferent to numbers and claim they don't miss the ecclesiastical machinery and its interest in statistics.

As I visited church leaders from different traditions, I had to be sensitive to what the concept of membership might mean. The term "unchurched" was broadened or narrowed in its meaning in the hope of finding people who had been outside of fellowship with the Church but were now active participants. For example, I called unchurched those Catholics who had been away from sacramental participation for five years or more. When such people made a move to reactivate their church membership, I felt that they were ripe for interviewing. But the definition had to be narrowed for some conservative Churches, where people might have attended for years before announcing their intention to become members. During those years of church related activity, these people could hardly be considered unchurched.

My working definition of unchurched for the purposes of this study was "persons who for at least five years were not members of a Church, or persons who, though on some membership list, did not attend worship services apart from holy days, and functions such as weddings, funerals, baptisms and confirmations." For these persons, the invitation "Let's go to church" had gotten a resounding "No, thanks." But some had changed their minds. I wanted to find out why.

2

Churches in Seven Counties

The connecting link among my seven counties was the statistical evidence that each had a population that was more than half unchurched. In most cases the county was in a wider region which also had a majority of people without church affiliation. But beyond that the counties were quite different. Four were predominantly rural, while three could be classified as metropolitan. They spanned the continent and were representative of the major regions of our country. In order to give some regional color, I have gathered together some impressions, brief snapshots of experiences, glimpses of church services and servers, and a sampling of the Churches' impact upon their communities.

POLK COUNTY, OREGON

Just a few weeks in Oregon convinces an easterner that the Oregonians are justifiably proud of their countryside. Nowhere else did I find such a love for the land. Young people, when asked, asserted that they wouldn't leave their home—as humble as it might be—for opportunity, advancement, or other supposed advantages elsewhere. With Salem, the nearby state capital, offering the ambiance of a small city, and the metropolitan atmosphere of Portland just an hour away, residents of Polk County (1975 population 38,928) do not feel that they are underprivileged because of any lack of cultural activities. The Oregon College of Education in Monmouth also adds a unique flavor to county life. The proximity of the Pacific coast westward and of mountain ranges east, west and south allows residents to point their cars and RVs in any direction for vacation wonderlands rarely equalled anywhere else. And the valley weather seems well insulated from extremes of heat and cold. The above average precipitation brings out the best in agriculture, if not in people. New arrivals stated that it takes a while to be able to enjoy the quiet peace and comfort of clouds and rain enough to make it through a wet period. For those who settle in the valley, the delight of mild days, orchards in flower and fruit, and the convenience of changes of scenery for leisure week ends more than compensate for the overly generous showers.

Where are the churches in Polk County, and how do they accent the lifestyle and landscape? An active Presbyterian layman said of Dallas, the county seat, "You can't throw a stone there without breaking a church window." In driving through Dallas, Monmouth, Independence, and the smaller towns, one sees both distinctive older churches, well cared for in most instances, and buildings of more recent vintage looking sturdy and winsome if not awe-inspiring. There is no lack of churches. Even very small towns boast modest buildings for adherents of two or three denominations. Bulletin boards give the bare-bones of activity announcements, while gaudier banners report Bible schools and upcoming social events.

But while many of the congregations worship comfortably in filled sanctuaries on Sunday mornings, other churches minister to small handfuls in buildings that enclose too much space. In Monmouth, First Christian continues to remodel to facilitate creative programs of activities for the growing congregation and also for community use. Some of the rooms are used daily by a group of retarded people from the area. A neighboring congregation shepherds a small circle of older members. A couple in their fifties, new to this church, found that they were almost the youngest people present on Sundays. Halfway between Monmouth and Independence, a congregation of the Lutheran Church-Missouri Synod worships in a functionally modern building, with plans for anticipated expansion. Two Baptist churches gave evidence through their new members of being warm and dedicated communities. However, the Presbyterian Church there, with falling membership, was forced to merge with the local Methodists to form Christ's Church. Although it is located on a hard-to-find side street, St. Patrick's Catholic Church has continued to grow under the leadership of its ecumenically-minded pastor.

In Dallas, many church buildings show the advantages of being situated in the county's main city. Downtown, First Presbyterian ministers to many of the area's leaders. In a strikingly modern plant, a large flock of Methodists gather. The Assembly of God congregation has an impressive new sanctuary on large acreage in an outlying section. But some of the town's churches show less success. The Church of the Foursquare Gospel is struggling, with barely 30 members in a small, older facility. The Evangelical Church of North America worships in a large building, but with a part-time ministry for a small group. Several branches of Mennonites are represented in large, attractive churches. Oft-repeated stories of splits in this established religious community are cited to explain of the proliferation of congregations from the original century-old Mennonite migrations to Polk County. The American Lutheran Church displays striking examples of modern religious art in its narthex. Sunday School buses can be seen resting during midweek in church parking lots. Behind the Christian and Missionary Alliance Church, a car parked in the same spot for several days announced via its bumper sticker that "In Case of Rapture, this Car will be Unmanned."

Add to these religious communities the smaller congregations of outlying towns, and there seems to be no shortage of churches. What factors, then, explain the unchurched rate of over 70 percent? The 40 or so churches in Polk County are so distributed that few people would find it difficult to go to a church. But less than 30 percent seem to care enough to declare membership. And this situation is hardly unique on the West Coast. Almost all the counties of the Pacific states show a population majority without church membership. A large number of these report over 70 percent unchurched.

From within the church establishment, pastors and church leaders try to find patterns of individual and community behavior which would explain the lack of interest in religious community and worship. One of the most capable pastors, an obvious leader, expressed concern that "the main reason for so many being unchurched is that no one has ever explained the Gospel to them." If that is true, does the fault lie with the Churches or with the unchurched? More important, how can that Gospel best be explained to those who have turned away? The pastor of a mainline church in Dallas, commenting on the change from his former parish in the Midwest, noted a "harshness, as a result of the marriage between frontier individualism and fundamentalistic religion."

What do the unchurched see when they look at the churches of Polk County? A lay leader in one of the Dallas congregations observed that the non-active draw the conclusion that: (1) the good people go to church on Sundays; (2) being a Christian means *not* doing things like smoking, drinking, playing cards; and (3) grace and redemption do not emerge from the Church's image. He described the church community as an "intensively religious community," claiming that such intensity, wedded to ethnicity, strict rules of behavior and a lack of interest in outsiders, forms an unattractive picture for the unchurched. A history buff claimed that the pioneers who settled in the Willamette Valley came in communities. There was a strict line between "ins" and "outs," he said, and the "ins" were dependent solely upon themselves. This was institutionalized in the development of religious groups. He continued, "So you have very religious people, and those who are outsiders. Church groups had come whose religion was a big part of their life. But their religion appeared to be a cultural ingroup that you had to buy into. They'll accept you in, if you buy the whole package." He then told of a Sikh, from India, who married a Mennonite girl and was converted. "You have never seen such a German, midwestern, Protestant ethic. He got about two and a half acres of land, he raises his own meat, has a big garden, and is always looking for a bargain. He works hard—and he's a Mennonite to the core."

Yet there is another side to the religious situation. There are parallels to the mild climate and gentle rain which make the fields abound also in the church atmosphere. The lack of traditions, the love of the land, the absence of striving and competition which we associate with older urban areas has for some helped the religious spirit to develop. Said ex-Michigander Don Kohl:

> We don't have all the people and the cars and the mass here that keep you from identifying with people or your community, or practicing your values openly. People still talk about religion. Take the July 4th parade. We were standing in line at the firehouse pancake breakfast and got to talking, and all of a sudden we're talking about this man's conversion with the Lord, and we're praising the Lord. You don't find that back East.

He described his church in Dallas, "That congregation and the Presbyterian Church is a loving Christian church, where, if you want to express the love of Christ in your life, you can do it. It appeals to me because we worship God through the Spirit but through our minds too. Its church government, and the way it makes decisions—that's my kind of process."

The love of the land and an appreciation for space and the beauty of the landscape also seem to help people express their love of the Church and its people. The phrases, "loving fellowship" and "community" were used more in Oregon than in the other counties. That openness and acceptance of other people that was found in some congregations, especially among the younger people, mark a particularly effective form of outreach. The formerly un-churched reported seeing in the lives of others an inner peace, "an ability to cope," a warmth, a "something different" that had the effect of drawing the unchurched into the target range of the Church's message.

What is the future shape of the Christian Church's presence in Polk County? People who work in Salem and even in cities to the south farther away have stated that they find in this semirural, small-town county a place to sink roots. Echoing the sentiments of commuters elsewhere, they claim it is worth the driving to work to be able to live in Dallas or Monmouth, Rickreall, or Buell, or even in isolated homes along the country roads, nestled in rolling fields, near orchards of cherries or filberts, or next door to a herd of brick-red Santa Gertrudis cattle. How will the churches minister to present residents of, or new migrants to this favored land? Can the loving communities, experienced now by few, draw others into their Christian fellowship? Will the suburban spill-over into West Salem on the eastern edge of the county cause an erosion of treasured small town ways? Or will it occasion new and vigorous church growth and an enrichment of the county's lifestyle?

One congregational evangelism group, thinking that the first step in their outreach plan was to find a way to listen to those outside the Church, studied *Who Are the Unchurched?* But they were the only church that reported such study, even though the book was written in part about people in their very own county. In Oregon, with its spirit of independence and self-sufficiency, evangelism may take a special shape. Only a few of the churches seem to be struggling with that challenge.

ORANGE COUNTY, CALIFORNIA

Under the heading "God's Business in Orange County," the local *Orange County Register* reported on three churches which have exerted a dominant influence on the religious scene. The success of these large Protestant congregations, the nonstop UHF Channel 40 of the Trinity Broadcasting Network inviting listeners to just "Praise the Lord," and the assorted witness of almost 400 additional churches of all denominations makes one hesitate to call Orange County in any way unchurched.

Yet, when asked whether it was true that the county had a larger number of unchurched people than elsewhere, one pastor answered, "I think that's true, at least visually it seems to be. I recall being in Houston a few times, where on Sunday morning you got up and looked outside and all the cars were starting to back out to take off for church. That certainly isn't what you observe here on a Sunday morning." His associate added, "Here it's three hours later, and they're backing out to go to the beach." An estimated 65 percent of the county's population (1978 population estimate was 1,768,000, an increase of over 20 percent since 1970) is not on any church roll, evidence that the pastor's perception was accurate.

Traveling across the county by expressways and eight lane arteries, one encounters a rich diversity of churches. There are the three large congregations referred to previously, Garden Grove Community Church, Melodyland Christian Center, and Calvary Chapel. Each is a growing congregation with 10,000 or more worshipers. Each exerts a powerful magnetic attraction far beyond its neighborhood. And each has a unique story.

The walk-in, drive-in Garden Grove Community Church has come a long way from the first religious service conducted from a snack-bar roof at the Orange Drive-In Theater. Robert H. Schuller, in the 23 years since that first service, has become surely one of the nation's best known religious leaders. The city of Garden Grove did not impress me as a particularly affluent community, yet Schuller was urged by local church leaders and, some say, also by the prestigious Norman Vincent Peale, a member of the same Reformed Church in America denomination, to get things started in that booming suburb. A layperson who conducted a tour of the sanctuary and "campus" after church on Sunday claimed that Dr. Schuller made 3,500 residential calls in those early years. Today a 14-story Tower of Hope, topped by a 90-foot lighted cross, is easily visible for miles around. In 1978 it overlooked the foundations for the new Crystal Cathedral which was under construction. I was impressed by the vigor of the well-administered congregation, by its devoted laity and varied programs, having previously known of the church only from its TV ministry called *Hour of Power*. When the Sunday bulletin lists a need for 300 new ushers, something must be going right. The five

families whom I interviewed from the church agreed enthusiastically.

The "possibility thinking" leadership, both clergy and lay, has
ministered to this congregation as a large number of subgroups,
many of them with a fellowship closer than might be found in a
typical small or medium-sized parish. Schuller also shares some
of his "know-how" with others who come from across the country
to his "Institute for Successful Church Leadership" seminars.
One of the parishioners stated that she and her husband have for
years offered a spare room to house one of the clerics attending
the week-long seminar. At first the participants express reserva-
tions about the promised results of the institute. But by the end of
the training sessions, in most cases, they are won over and join
the 5,300 other alumni, sharing the Schuller maxims that "God's
biggest problem is getting you to think something is possible" and
"the Church can grow as long as there are unchurched people."

Another pastor, in a different corner of Orange County, and
from a dissimilar religious background, Ralph Wilkerson, can recall his humble beginning nearly 20 years ago as he began ministering with 20 followers in 1960. Wilkerson is the undisputed
leader of a conglomerate of religious agencies known as the
Melodyland Christian Center in Anaheim, just a short distance
from the entrance to Disneyland. After ten years his congregation had grown so large that six services were held each Sunday in
its 900-seat building. Then he became aware that Melodyland, a
theater-in-the-round that had fallen into financial difficulties,
might be for sale. Wilkerson's church found itself the only bidder,
making the purchase for just over a million dollars. Today it offers
facilities for a school of theology, a Christian high school, hot-line
and counseling services and the varied needs of an estimated
12,000 "signed members."

My impressions were mixed after visiting the Melodyland complex. The waiting room was bustling with people who wanted to
meet one of the officials. The hallway of offices was guarded by a
clanking iron door. There was a slickness to the procedures that
made me feel ill at ease. But over the weekend I attended a musi-

cal, the "Story of Pentecost," that showed me another side to
Melodyland. It was a musical extravaganza presented in the
former theater that traced God's work in the Church, beginning
with the disciples in Jerusalem and continuing with the reforma-
tions of Luther and Wesley. "A Mighty Fortress" was sung in soft
rock by a large chorus with full orchestral accompaniment. The
new Pentecostal experience at Azusa Street, Los Angeles, was de-
picted, as was the Catholic renewal of Vatican II and the charismatic activity within the Church beginning at Notre Dame. Wilkerson spoke briefly at the close about the reverberations of the
first Pentecost, and with the aid of professional lighting and
sound equipment he gave some indication of why Melodyland has
experienced such dramatic growth.

I had visited Calvary Chapel, in Costa Mesa, during the week
and spoken to Pastor Romaine, one of the nine pastoral leaders.
He suggested that I attend worship service on Sunday morning
and then interview some of the parishioners to whom he would
introduce me. The attractive facilities are so unobtrusive that I
had driven by them without realizing that the church was there.
But I had heard of Calvary Chapel wherever I went, even from a
young woman attending Calvary whom I remembered from
Lutheran Sunday School in my first parish in Columbus, Ohio.
Unlike most churches, Calvary Chapel has a large number of people who attend services and classes but retain membership in
Catholic or Protestant congregations elsewhere. They attend for
a variety of reasons: fellowship, Bible study, vigorous preaching,
special programs or just because of the up-beat worship. I went to
early service on Sunday morning. The building was filled with
about 2,500 worshipers. After they filed out, arrangements began
for the next influx. Overflow crowds at the second service sat on
the edge of the planters scattered around the grounds, listening to
the service on loudspeakers. I was introduced to three young adults
whom I interviewed in the prayer room. Pastors were counseling
with individuals around us as I questioned these formerly unchurched people. When the interview was over and the young people had left, I found myself alone—except for one young man sitting

in the corner with his Bible open on his lap. I introduced myself to him, apologized for our loud talking, and sat down. His name was Tim. He said that, as was his custom, he attended the same early service that I had, then came to the prayer room to ask God's blessings upon the speaker and the hearers at the second service, who were worshiping just beyond the wall of the prayer room. I began to talk with him, with tape-recorder on, and it turned out to be one of my best interviews.

In Tim's account, Calvary Chapel was born through the unlikely cooperation of Jesus people—called freaks by some, and too unkempt to be welcomed into other congregations—and young people, like himself ten years ago, who had fallen into the use of hard drugs but were trying to get out. Under the leadership of Pastor Chuck Smith, Calvary Chapel ministered to these and other young folk. Personal witness, sharing, inviting were the means of growth from that handful of young people into a religious institution that keeps radiating Christian fervor and devotion even beyond the borders of Orange County. Every year large crowds of people are baptized in the ocean at Corona del Mar.

In addition to worship and study programs, religious rock concerts are a regular Saturday evening feature. The congregation is totally independent, yet it has spawned perhaps 50 other Calvary Chapels in the Southwest, and is spreading farther afield. Events at the church form only one part of a varied ministry. The operation includes a Christian academy and produces books, records, radio programs and handcrafted Christian jewelry, offering employment to new adherents. A fellow pastor and I puzzled over the secret of such success. Smith's preaching is effective but low-key, we agreed. The music and original twists in the worship service are pleasant, often delightful. But still it isn't readily apparent to us why so many have turned to Calvary Chapel. Tim knows.

In addition to these three congregations, there are about 45 Catholic parishes, with memberships averaging nearly 7,000. The newly-instituted Diocese of Orange County is appraising the possibilities open to it in America's fastest growing county. The large Spanish-speaking population is a special responsibility. A Spanish priest noted that there were in Orange County 45 barrios of Chicano residents and that most Catholic churches had Spanish-speaking priests and services. "Their concept of membership might not be so strict," he said. "Almost all of them are baptized. But I imagine a good number are non-practicing Catholics. They are more cultural Christians." When I asked him if he had any formal program of outreach, his answer reflected the reality expressed by many other priests, "No ... We have enough troubles—enough work just taking care of those who do try to keep up their affiliation." But another priest emphasized a new program to tap the "time and talents" of "every single Catholic family in the county of Orange." A form was being circulated listing almost 90 volunteer tasks and requesting recruits from the Catholic population.

Yet somewhere near a million county residents choose not to be counted as members of any church. Many are housed behind walls that extend for blocks and screen expensive homes from speeding traffic. They are part of a bustling growth that some say will turn Orange County into another Los Angeles. Airports, office buildings, and the ubiquitous shopping centers are filled with fashionable types that would be at home on Wilshire Boulevard fifty miles away or across the continent on Park Avenue. Retirement communities are elegant, and the miles of beach support a whole sub-industry. Universities and colleges dot the landscape. And there seems to be so much more land to be developed for the future.

Some of my interviewees implied that the predominant feeling of Orange County people was "playtime, all the time." Others blamed the "transplant syndrome" affecting those migrants who come to escape from responsibility. They often find no sense of community, but rather practice an anonymous lifestyle which lets them vacation from their Church indefinitely. More than one interviewee said he felt that his family was the only one on the street that attended church. Yet, that big cross over Garden Grove sheds its light a long distance, and the Calvary Chapel faithful—who seem to be full of more youthful vigor than any other church—will make sure that the flower they have planted in Orange County will flourish.

WALDO COUNTY, MAINE

The tourist promotional material for Maine speaks glowingly of "Your Four-Season Vacationland," but the natives warn that winter wins the major victory. After too short a summer, they say, there are three months preparing for winter, four months enduring it, and three more months cleaning up after it. But I found early fall a delight in Waldo County. Although the days were mild, I had to take a blanket from the motel to wrap around me during an evening tent revival. I looked around at the sparse crowd and saw that everyone else was dressed for winter—on September 8. Hearing a description of the stiff winter of 1977-78, I wondered if the term "cabin fever" originated in Maine. The more well-to-do parishioners go to Florida every winter, pastors reported. Even natives with historical origins in the area have begun to think seriously about moving south.

The town of Belfast, the "shiretown," was settled by Scotch-Irish. The name Belfast revives old country memories. When the British closed in on the town during the Revolutionary War, these Presbyterians scattered. When they returned, often from New Hampshire, they brought back Congregationalists with them. Thus the First Church was developed as a Congregational church. Through this historic quirk the county does not have a Presbyterian congregation in keeping with its origins.

According to *Churches and Church Membership 1971* Waldo County (1975 population 26,187) is over 80 percent unchurched. It has the distinction of the highest incidence of unchurched in the entire Northeast. In addition, Waldo and its eastern neighbor county are the only New England counties where no one denomination has as much as 25 percent of the churched. Congregations are small, the average being about 100 confirmed members.

The largest parish seems to be the Catholic Church of St. Francis in Belfast. Set apart from most of the other churches, it ministers to traditional adherents. The pastor reported no new members who were formerly unchurched. The state itself counts 61 percent of its churched population as Catholic. Protestant churches of the major denominations are found in most towns of Waldo County and are often housed in imposing colonial style structures. Some of the churches are "union" or "federated," that is, the result of merging two or more congregations. Some have a pastor from a denomination different from that of the congregation. I saw newly-painted white church buildings set on a rise in the land, commanding a view of the village or bay, with entrance road winding down and tall steeple pointing upward—the stuff of post cards and Christmas pictures.

On Sunday mornings the scene may look less romantic. In one of the main Belfast churches, the single service I attended was less than half full. The average age must have been almost 55 years. The Sunday School numbered less than 100. The young, determined pastor led a dignified worship service. A Baptist church in town had midweek Bible study for a handful. One member reported that the repair of the picturesque old steeple taxed their budget severely. Several miles to the east, the apparently fastest growing congregation in the county, Searsport Full Gospel, fills the church both in the morning and again in the evening. Despite unsuccessful attempts to provide parochial education in their own school, the congregation plans to enlarge its outreach with a bus ministry.

One of the county's ministers, admittedly a "Maine-iac," had some doubts about Waldo County's unique position as the most unchurched in the state. But he confessed that it could be true partly because the "ministers who serve in this area are perhaps men who are thinking of retirement and have given their better years elsewhere. Or they are just young, inexperienced men out of the seminary and using churches in Waldo County as a stepping-stone to a larger church." A second reason given was, "The evangelicals, years gone by, have had a ministry that we would call a 'burnt over' policy, whereby they have preached hell and judgment and brimfire to the extent that people have been turned against the church . . . and have hardened themselves." Another factor was suggested: "The Church in Waldo County, like the Church every-where, is under the strict and severe judgment of God because we have not left the walls of our buildings and gone out to visit with the people in their homes to struggle with their problems and feel their pain and hurt. Perhaps this last reason is the greatest—that we are not committed to a biblical and a strong, loving outreach, as we should be."

What factors make Waldo County different from other areas in the region? One clergyman said that while there was an increase of population because of young people fleeing the cities, these newcomers are not always welcome. The fear is that these people will want to bring their ideas and change the way of living for older residents, he suggested. Some pointed to the attitudes re-vealed in the traditional town meetings as a symbol of the con-flict. Another problem is that Belfast, while an attractive area to live in, offers little available housing. "For Sale" signs are stuck in the lawns, but they usually advertise old Greek revival "captains' houses," complete with "widow's walk," which would not suit the needs or the resources of young couples just starting out. Trailer courts, in contrast, are also nearby. Some of the more adventurous county folk seek older farms in little communities like Morrill, Unity and Winterport.

An unusual example is a young couple living down a country road, about a mile from the nearest neighbor, in a hand-hewn, log faced house. They are new members of a Belfast church. But their pastor warned that I would not be able to telephone them for an interview. "They take the telephone jack out after they're finished calling, so that other people can't call in to disturb them," he said. "They feel that a telephone is only for calling out."

One senses a cautious reserve, almost a shyness, about the peo-ple. Does this carry over to their church life? Does the rugged, independent Mainer find it hard to reach out to newcomers? Does it take an emotionally-charged worship style to defrost people who have lived long "at the end of the road?" How do the churches fare? One pastor wondered aloud about the unwillingness of his members to evangelize. He asked, was it because "there's a great deal of bashfulness about it? Or because of the stereotype of the

New England great respect for not pushing one's religion on someone else?"

Considering the decline in religious observance, one of the
younger pastors suggested reasons not that much different from
what other pastors say elsewhere: "I think that people are seeing
the Church as not being able to compete with other measures of
entertainment. For those who are looking for that kind of thing, I
don't think the Church is able to pull it off as well as the shows
they see on TV all the time. People who grew up on farms were
away from the center of town. Apparently they were relatively
comfortable with being quiet, really decent people. But they were
not so much joiners."

One pastor pointed out the history of doctrinal differences
between the Churches and the people, and among the Churches
themselves. A liberal Protestant, he felt that "what religion there
is in this area tends to be fairly conservative." The large United
Church of Christ congregation in Belfast had an affinity, histori-
cally, with the Unitarian congregation. In recent years the two
were united. A conservative Baptist splinter group occupied the
Unitarian building. The pastor of First Church, Belfast, Rev. Doug
Showalter, suggested that one class of churchgoer is more concerned with critically, rationally examining religion, while another
operates more at the emotional end of the spectrum. He continued:

> I feel fairly strongly that a lot of people are looking for solid
> answers to faith. Someone like Billy Graham can get up and
> talk about heaven and hell and sin and righteousness; and he
> can set it forth in a very clearcut way which people can find
> very appealing. It doesn't take an awful lot of intellectual
> understanding. It's something that people can pick right off
> the top and find meaning in it. It's much easier to say some-
> thing is absolutely wrong or absolutely right, and to have peo-
> ple follow it and get worked up about it, than it is to tell
> someone, "Well, in this circumstance, it's so and so." The
> denomination I represent tends to probably gray the issues, to
> see more grays. The liability there is the fact that people
> don't get emotionally grabbed about the issues and sometimes
> don't even take the time to find out what they are. They just

figure that they can't understand it, so why bother to come to any conclusion? I think there are different approaches, and I think it's a real task in my denomination to get people emotionally involved. Too often there can be an intellectual adherence to a series of tenets.

One of the more conservative pastors, Roger Merrill, also felt that clear preachments were what the people were looking for. He approached the challenge of his ministry in the Nazarene Church in Belfast with a surprising confidence. "I anticipate within the next two years doubling my membership," he said, and continued:

I really believe our secret is people involvement; realizing that I'm the pastor, but it's their ministry. It's catching on. People aren't sitting back, waiting to be chosen. They're saying, "Well, I think I have this ability in this area. Is there something that I can do?" When you have people being involved, the Church is being built on people and their circle of friends.... I believe that our appeal is in endeavoring to live what we profess to have. We do not demand any signs of being spiritual except the way we live, where our spiritual lives have become actually more important than anything else. First we're Christian, and then we are whatever we are after that. We're a Christian janitor, or a Christian minister, or what have you.

When asked why he felt unchurched people should consider joining his congregation, he answered, "My total congregation right now is searching for something solid to hang on to. Because of that searching, they are becoming grounded in Christ, in the word of God. I think the strong points are the loving people who are really searching for something that means security in this life and a hope of a future life."

One of the Methodist pastors, described by some people as the best preacher in town, found the cultural shock in moving to Waldo County more stimulating than discouraging. While admitting the "genuine indifference toward the Church even within the Churches," he spoke appreciatively of the "real open honesty." "If people don't want anything to do with the Church, they tell you, 'I don't want anything to do with the Church. Now if there is any possibility that you and I can have any kind of relationship apart from that, fine—I want to be your friend. But. . . .' And even those within the Church, if they have a problem with me, I hear it from them, not from Mrs. Smith who said that Mrs. Jones said that. . . ."

However, that honesty can also be unbending, the minister found. He said, "These people have almost a fear of any kind of outreach program. They won't do it—even with their own kind of people." When he described the goal of evangelism to the congregation and defined it as reaching the unreached, bringing the Church to the unchurched, he reported the people said, "Fine, pastor, you do it. That's your job. . . . We don't know how to go to talk to other people. And, well, it wouldn't do any good anyway." Yet this same pastor felt that there is a little closing of that social distance and some outreach:

> It's not through a lot of intensive kind of personal one-to-one thing. Someone has said to outsiders, "Why don't you come to our church?" or they happened in off the street. Or I meet them in another context and they say, "Hey, I like you. Maybe I'll come to church some Sunday and hear what you have to say." And they come back. Some of them may say, "Stop by. . . . We'd like to sit and chat like this." It's been a slow process . . . but I think there's a trend there.

For the sake of Waldo County's churched and unchurched, I hope that this vigorous young minister and others like him will be willing to put in more years and see these new processes begin to bear fruit.

BOONE COUNTY, WEST VIRGINIA

The colors were just beginning to turn on the hillsides as I entered Boone County (1975 population: 27,858) after leaving Charleston. The main town and county seat is Madison. In late afternoon, a mini-traffic jam ties up the one main street. Many of the people look old and worn. There are stern, wrinkled faces that even brightly-colored polyester sport jackets or pastel pant suits can't soften. Just two miles away from Madison, a heavy concentration of railroad tracks and cars fills in the western edge of Danville. Long coal trains, including heavy-equipment carriers, begin to move in the early morning hours. Frequently the main road runs parallel to the tracks, instead of involving frequent inconvenient crossings. Boone County may not be the very heart of coal-country, but the economy of the county is built solidly on coal. And of course when the coal mines strike, many things stop. One minister told me that "everybody who's been in the mines five years knows someone who's been killed in the mines." Maybe it is that harsh history that is written in deep lines across the faces of Madison's shoppers.

Traveling down one of the winding roads that cross the county, one finds a number of churches—mostly small—of varying denominations. Madison Baptist, Bible Baptist in Danville, St. Joseph in Whitesville, Ashford Church of God Holiness, Madison Methodist, and several of the Churches of Christ have impressive buildings. They appear sturdy, growing, prosperous. Small chapels can be seen on the state roads. And there are signs pointing to still others along the narrow lanes that lead up into the hills.

I tried to visit the clergy, but found that many are "bi-vocational," which means that they are only parttime in their pastoral work. Some are miners the rest of the time. Wednesday evening service at the Nazarene Church that I attended was conducted by a layman because the mining shift came up too late for the preacher to arrive in time to take charge. This lack of full-time, well-trained church leaders was suggested as one cause for the high percentage of unchurched in Boone County. But one of the town pastors also noted that sometimes well-educated pastors are neither welcome nor effective. "There are pockets where education is frowned upon, really," he said. "If you're an educated person, you lose rapport with some of these people.... Just the way you talk, and your actions, cause some to turn you off right there." The kind of religious expression to be found in Appalachia depends upon who is making the evaluation. A mainline Baptist pastor said, "I think these people are won more by emotionalism than they are by teaching. They find the routine of organized church very—how shall I say it—not as interesting to them as when there's a lot of excitement, a lot of loud singing." Another pastor, who moved down from the North, observed, "I think it's worse here because the people are more primitive." Although he approved the opening up of the county by new roads and even a modern expressway, he felt that this also put a new emphasis on "entertainment . . . something which they didn't have before."

I found a style of religious expression that can best be called "old-fashioned." It is a mixture of bias and naiveté—with more than a grain of truth. For instance, it was not uncommon to hear people say, "The schools are teaching evolution in many ways. That's putting people against the Bible." There was evidenced a defensiveness against new moral standards or the lack of them. But statements could be so cliché-ridden and out of touch that one might wonder how effective such moralizing could be. Said one leader:

> There's been some new cult movements, Jesus freaks they call themselves, Children of God. But I believe that the hippy movement, a lot of them, because of what they're advocating, is maybe worse. They're teaching free love, anything goes, the new morality. I know some preachers who tried to work with them, and they would display a very gross attitude toward someone.

This same fundamentalist preacher also fired broadsides at the "generation gap, liberalism, the ecumenical movement, denominationalism—and other preachers—becoming comedians, magicians." He gave as evidence for his views reports of an assortment of bizarre pulpit antics in Churches other than that of the speaker's own fellowship. A Church of Christ pastor offered one solution—set up debates:

> Preachers won't meet and they won't debate issues. There used to be a lot of religious debates. We still love that, and the people like it too. I could have a debate over here in the high school gym or somewhere and it would be full. People would go for that. Finding somebody—that's our problem—finding somebody who would debate. I've challenged several people here but they usually turn us down. But a debate al-

ways fills a building because there's two preachers with opposing views. It seems like people are interested in hearing two other people debate because they seem to lack nerve to get up themselves, to defend what they believe. People usually say, "Well, we decided that debating docs more harm than good." That depends on whether you win or lose the debate.

The Presbyterians support a mission venture called the West Virginia Mountain Project. They fill a void with their distinctive theology and approach. According to the Rev. Harry Palmer in Ridgeview, pastor of a three-point parish, "One of the sayings around here is: 'If you want religion, you go to the little sect churches, but if you want help, you go to the Presbyterian Church.'" He explained the special need people have in battling fires. The fire station nearest him is 12 miles away. House fires, he claimed, usually result in a complete loss. "They occur at night. What usually happens is people escape with their lives and that's it. So one of the things I have on hand is sheets and blankets. These are new things, not rummage sale. So that if there is a fire in the area, I can load some things in my car and be there with immediate help." His concern is also expressed by calling on anyone in the community who is in the hospital. Since a large number of the pastors are bi-vocational, often only weekend lay preachers, the hospital visitation is considered a needed and effective ministry.

The Ashford Church of God (Holiness) pastor, John Hathaway, was most cooperative. In advance of my arrival, he offered to send me the names of several families who fit the criteria for the former unchurched. Pastor of a very conservative congregation, he was both ecumenically involved with the other churches and aggressive in his outreach. The people whom I visited from his parish talked of their conversion in terms of a change from darkness to light, from despair to hope, from damnation to the joy of salvation. Along with this, they said, came a willingness to submit to the strict moral laws of the Church. Yet stopping in the church at an off hour I found a group of young people with instruments and sophisticated sound equipment, readying themselves for some program. The music was good and the young people seemed to be enjoying it fully. Apparently featuring this variety of music in a conservative church offered no problems.

Visits to other special music programs in the area included a real gospel music bash in the auditorium at Madison. I estimated that well over a thousand people had paid five dollars each for tickets. There was a satisfying combination of other-worldly theology with well-played, professionally-packaged music. The audience got into the hand-clapping with such gusto that the commercial show seemed almost like a big tent meeting. Hawkers were advertising records and tapes and other souvenirs during the intermission. Many walked out with handfuls of such items.

One pastor noted another bit of evidence pointing to the deep and wide religious underpinnings of the community:

> People talk religion so freely. Because there's no front license plate, there are many cars that have "Jesus Saves" or "Christ Is The Answer" or something of that sort. There is this type of Bible Belt piety so that you do have a little different basis for working than I found more particularly in New England, where there was such a blasé attitude about religion.

The proliferating little churches up in the hills are set back along the winding roads that follow meandering streams. They are often filled with people bound by family ties. When asked if he thought Boone County was more highly unchurched than other areas, a young pastor said: "If you would drive up into the hollows and around the 1250 square miles, I would say, 'Yes.' Despite all the tiny churches that you would see, all the people in Boone County could never get into them."

The fact that there is a lot of inter-marrying among the church members means that when families have a feud they may also found a new church. It is not hard to find people who have been associated with many different churches of different denominations during their lifetime. Also the electronic church has a special appeal. One of the clergy observed, "I believe a lot of people get their church on the radio or TV. It's very convenient for them. They don't have to leave the hollow, come down that beat-up road, go down into where it's a local community thing. Maybe they are at odds with that relative or neighbor."

Revivals play an important part in religious experience here. During my visit, the Danville Church of Christ was advertising a revivalist well-known to the community. The preacher told me he felt that many would come and be saved during the last days of a week-long program. From the mainline Churches' point of view, the revival may be good for only a short-lived religious jolt, part of a "numbers game" of counting up "how many are saved" that does not help build a sustained community. In contrast, many interviewees reported that a long-lasting change did begin with revival. When these people were unchurched, they found it easier and less threatening to attend a revival than a regular worship service. More than one person said, "Church service is for after you get saved." Because of the demanding moral precepts involved, many people delayed church membership, but considered themselves Christian.

What direction, what trends can one identify in church life? The two young priests at the two-point Catholic parish in Whitesville and Madison, separated by 30 miles, are optimistic. They report that some, even from the local area, have overcome deep-seated prejudice and found community in a Catholic congregation. Said Fr. Bruno Bugascz, "There's a real sense of 'Look, we hunted around from Church to Church. We know what's in all those Churches. We've come here—this is where we want to be. We've chosen this, we know what's here.'" Fr. Jonathan Williams added, "I don't think we use the word Catholic as much as we see our mission very much as just really treating people to the Gospel. That is just something that people love to hear, but they can hardly believe it...that God loves them unconditionally. Gospel love and mercy of God—you can just sense the presence of the Spirit and the delight...." Their deep involvement in the community is symbolized by their living quarters in Madison, a mobile home in the middle of a large trailer park.

In spite of disparate backgrounds, there is some ecumenical cooperation. The Presbyterian, Catholic, Church of God (Holiness), Methodist and Baptist congregations in Madison conduct joint Thanksgiving and Easter sunrise services. Perhaps more importantly, they share and have grown together in their ministries. One of their number summed up well a goal I think they would all strive for, "I think we've got to do something to let people have a religious experience, a religious experience that draws them into the community and then is nurtured and fed by that community. You can just see people at peace with their Church—no, not with their Church, but with their experience with God."

Boone County is a landscape of contrasts I discovered. The fast-food companies, ever-present in other corners of our country, have not penetrated deeply into it. (I must admit to patronizing one Dairy Queen in Danville.) But there was a note of irony in a "No Trespassing" sign in glowing red that I spotted, nailed up over a dilapidated garage which seemed to house nothing of any value to anyone. A large warehouse was identified as the Independent Explosives Co. Chickens were running loose from coops precariously perched on such steep hillsides that I wondered if half the eggs rolled down out of the nests. An unruly troop of wrecked auto hulks could be seen scattered askew with no parking lines to discipline them. There were rugged outcroppings of jagged rock, with no softening fern or ivy. One of the conservative young preachers had a hang-glider sail furled outside his house. Some of the people looked like badly-cared-for dolls. Fine English features could be detected on a face too thin or too fat, with bad teeth, a poor color, and the look of inadequate nutrition. Yet I saw an admirable hardiness in some eyes, and a solid integrity that —even though it can be wrong-headed at times—is a rare asset.

On a rainy, chilly evening, the Moline (Methodist) Chapel was filled with folks caught in the spell of two singing groups which tour the area. The pastor was out for the first day of squirrel hunting and thereby considered excused. The lay leader welcomed all warmly. He was so emotionally moved during the music that he had a hard time introducing the players. He pointed into the audience to one younger man and remembered—for everyone—the time when Charlie had made his decision. He had walked out into the aisle, had fallen on his knees and, unable to walk, had crawled to the altar. A life was changed, fears replaced by a sense of joy and peace—in church.

MARION COUNTY, ALABAMA

Perhaps Patrick Breheny, pastor of the Catholic Church of the Holy Spirit in Winfield, Alabama, had a sense of déjà vu as another Lutheran pastor from up North parked his car in the rectory driveway. If he had an impulse to flinch, he never let on; he treated me with the same warm hospitality he had accorded Russell Hale two years earlier. I learned that Fr. Pat, one of his seminarian assistants, and a neighboring priest-colleague call Long Island home, as I do. Most of the Catholics connected with the parish seem to come from somewhere else. Many of them are apparently so satisfied with their new Alabama home that they are considering staying for good.

Holy Spirit is just one—but the only Catholic one—of an estimated 80 congregations in Marion County, in the northwest corner of Alabama about 80 miles from Birmingham. But that's a lot more than *Churches and Church Membership 1971* reports. Many churches, including some of good size, do not report membership to any national denomination and therefore would have fallen through the net of the 1971 national study. The 20 or more Churches of Christ, for example, take pride in reporting to no one, but guard their independence fiercely and consider the lack of national statistical information a small price to pay for their autonomy. Likewise, many of the 50 or more Baptist churches are not affiliated with any conference. CCM would also have omitted some of them. Ecumenical sharing is limited in the county to necessary chores like lining up preachers for a regular radio program. Only those with roots elsewhere express disappointment in not having a more regular ministerial fellowship. Independence is an accepted posture.

Blacks account for about 2.5 percent of the county's population of 27,119 (1975 count). They are clustered in three or four small communities and are in the lower economic bracket.

One of the most impressive churches, to me, is the Guin Free Will Baptist. In addition to nurturing a large and active congregation, it sponsors the Liberty Christian School, one of a system of evangelical schools country-wide. The staff is uniformed in red, white and blue. The students are neatly dressed—and look about as happy as most school kids. Pastor Richard R. Cordell is certainly a most impressive church leader. He can dream dreams and share those dreams with his people. He offered plenty of names of formerly unchurched persons to visit and interview. Each of them expressed an enthusiasm for the Gospel, the congregation and the pastor, not always in that order. I attended the Sunday church service on their "Old-Fashioned Day," which featured horses and buggies, hoop skirts and winged collars. Everyone seemed to participate, including the pastor with his narrow-waisted coat. Pastor Cordell said of his church, "We would not appeal to the nominal church member, or the person who was interested in being a nominal church member. But we do appeal to the folks who are interested in getting down to business for God, being saved, born again, living a changed life."

The preacher at the Guin Church of Christ gave me a carefully-worded historical sketch of that interesting religious movement. Their national membership is estimated at over two million. They are linked by common historic roots with the million or so members of the Christian Churches and Churches of Christ and with the more liberal million-plus members of the Christian Church (Disciples of Christ). But the non-instrumental branch, which prohibits piano or organ from being used in church, as represented in Guin, has chosen a more conservative and independent course. These people are biblical fundamentalists; some would say literalistic. They have no denominational or ecumenical connection. Preacher Jim Mullican described the "restoration principle" as distinctly different from the "reformation principle" that guides most Protestant Churches. He claimed that the Churches of the Reformation:

> still had not gone all the way back. They were still wearing names that were not in the Bible. . . . As a result of [our early leaders'] activities, we just call ourselves Christians, not Baptist, Methodists, or whatever. That we ought to practice just what the Bible teaches, not add to it or take from it. That there was no clergy in the Bible, all believers were just Christians, each one on an equal basis with the other. As

a result of this they began preaching the idea of restoring the New Testament Church.

Interestingly enough he could produce no names of new members who were formerly unchurched.

Believing that the Church of Christ's principles are unique has led to inviting members of other denominations to join the "true Church." While admitting that this draws a line between Churches of Christ and other Churches and often results in misunderstanding and even resentment, the preacher said:

> We only feel that Christ established one Church. If we are not practicing what He taught, then we can't claim to be part of His Church. And so we believe that if the same seed which we still have in the New Testament is planted today, the Christians resulting and the churches that result will be the same as the ones in the first century. If the seed is pure, then the Church will be.

The town of Guin shows a surprisingly impressive set of church buildings. After the tornado of a few years back, the congregations had to rebuild. Likewise, Hamilton and Winfield have large, attractive and apparently successful churches. But outside of these towns, and smaller communities like Hackleburg and Brilliant, there are many people living along rural roads. Churches out in the country are few and humble in structure. Two of the pastors I visited to get background material and the names of potential interviewees were willing to admit that they themselves were formerly unchurched. Of course I interviewed them!

With all its church buildings, why is Marion County included among the counties with larger than average proportions of unaffiliated people? We must acknowledge at least a superficial contact with biblical religion on the part of a large number of residents in this Bible Belt county. Yet even if we add the members of the independent congregations, including the Churches of Christ, churchgoers are still in the minority. Could one of the problems lie with the Churches themselves? When we were talking about the radio preachers who continually play inspirational music, and conduct worship and bible study, one of the clergy protested,

"Surely the knowledge of Christianity is really dismal. And some of the effects of lack of quality religious education are found in the early marriages, divorces, child abuse. Care for the poor and the quality of education are low too." As far as the churches' involvement in social issues is concerned, he continued, "They care for their own. As far as appreciating the social dimension of Christianity, it isn't there. As far as cooperation goes—that's bad too."

But many of the out-of-staters who transferred from headquarters far away down to industrial plants in Marion County remark that they find the people to be very genteel, the pace slower and the climate better. The hard-nosed laws against liquor turn some off, but there are ways of getting around those rules. The youth are preoccupied with school and athletics. One pastor complained, "What they do have is sports, and that is almost a god here." Dancing is prohibited in the churches and frowned upon elsewhere. A recent attempt to establish a disco in Winfield was opposed by the churches. A pastor appeared at the town board meeting to make known his disapproval and that of his conservative congregation. It was one of the few social issues that the church got concerned about, I was told.

Some of the clergy readily admit their strict opposition to dancing, movies, rock music, pants on women, long hair on men, and television. One pastor put it this way:

> We believe in separation from the world. Without separation, I don't think you have any anointing. I don't think God's anointing is just on any organization. I think it's in the standard, the dedication. You have His power then to be better witnesses. I strongly believe this and stress this. It's not a hobby horse we could get off. We do have a standard. I don't want to Christianize a person when they don't live according to a standard as others do.

The Catholic parish includes five counties. Catholics number only about 275 in a total population of 100,000. It is estimated that 40 percent of them do not attend Mass. An associate pastor works from a residence in the northern counties, while Fr. Pat Breheny lives in Winfield. Two religious sisters administer an educational

program and another sister coordinates social concerns. Two semi-
narians assist, particularly in youth ministry. The small congregation that meets in the sanctuary in Winfield shows a close
fellowship and a gratitude for their Church's ministries.

One of the Baptist clergy told me about a favorite youth activity
in Winfield on Friday and Saturday nights:

> They have what they call "riding the loop." Come all the way
> through town; it's a continuous thing. The kids just ride and
> then they park on the street. And you'll find a thousand to-
> morrow night. . . . And it's amazing to watch—silly—but that's
> teenagers for you. They set on the hood of the cars. They park
> vertically along the streets and the parking lots and wave at
> everybody as they go by. Then they'll get in the car and they'll
> drive around a while, and they'll wave. It's just a fad, but
> it's one thing that's been here. And it'll continue to be here;
> they enjoy doing it. One generation to the 'nother. And of
> course, there's some things that goes on down there that's not
> good.

But there's also one thing that is pretty good. A group of young
people run "The Open Door," a Christian coffeehouse sponsored
by several Churches of God of Prophecy. I visited them one evening and chatted for a while. The next evening I brought my tape
recorder along and, over *Dr. Peppers* and *7-Ups*, interviewed five
or six out of the dozen. They are now in their twenties and actively
involved in their church life, although for several years they were
unchurched. After talking for almost an hour—including sharing
some pretty heavy remembrances—they broke into song. "This
Little Gospel Light of Mine" was served up with some great
barrelhouse piano, tambourine and guitar. So a few at least have
found an alternative to "riding the loop."

SARASOTA COUNTY, FLORIDA

I found it hard not to fall in love with Sarasota County in November, enjoying sunny days and blue skies while back home it was
dark and chilly. I also found some pretty exciting people who
were more than willing to share with me their experiences as
formerly unchurched. The Rev. Charles Bruce, pastor of Trinity

United Methodist Church in North Port, on the lower edge of the county, said, "Florida is not a southern state, although it's the southernmost state in the U.S. It is a cosmopolitan state; there are more people from the Northeast. My church is composed largely of people out of Indiana, Ohio, New York and Pennsylvania." When asked about the Church's potential in this area, he commented, "Beautiful, fantastic! I'm enthused about the fantastic opportunity here. Because all I got to do is stand out here with a butterfly net and do a fairly decent job, and this church is going to be increased." This is a very modest statement by a capable cleric who puts much effort into sermon and church program—much more than swinging a butterfly net.

Local brochures claim that Sarasota County experienced a growth from 1970 to 1974 of 32 percent, rating second in the nation. Population is given in two figures: residential at 183,000 (1978 estimate) and functional, peak season, which assumes that all dwelling units are occupied, at 220,000. But *Churches and Church Membership 1971* notes that only 39.9 percent of this burgeoning population was counted on church membership roles.

Some clerical leaders concur in this assessment. Others are still smarting from the publicity given to Russell Hale's study of the unchurched and its claim that a majority of the county's population are in that category.

One pastor said, describing the "Florida Syndrome":

I used to think it was just the Church, and I have discovered through my associations and conversations that it concerns virtually every organization—that is, civic clubs, fraternal orders, and churches. People retire from Indiana; they come to Florida, and they retire with a capital "R". Whatever they did, wherever they came from, they're not going to do it here. "No, built a church in Indianapolis, not going to do that anymore. Went to church school and church all my life: I'm retired now." And I mean they retired—period. They pick up new activities, substitute activities. . . . They are more active in many respects than they were during the period that they were working. But whatever they did where they came from, they don't want to do now, because they associate that with work. They're retired now. It's as if they stepped across some invisible line and totally changed their lifestyle.

One of the functions of the Churches in Sarasota County, as seen by a church leader, is to be an agent of reconciliation between the seniors—retired, enjoying leisure-centered living—and the very much younger people who work as a support community: police, fire-fighters, and those who run motels, restaurants, gas stations and tourist shops. In this somewhat artificial setting, there is a dearth of those in the middle years, between 35 and 55. Can the Church help to overcome the barriers, somehow to say that the two groups' needs are not mutually exclusive and that they really need one another? Another problem is the rootless condition of many who migrated south. They may have left behind families, grandchildren, life-long friends, all the support systems and groups that helped to make life hang together. Can these people— old or young, but especially the older—find new community?

Some of the Churches, in trying to express community, use different categories of membership to accommodate people who spend up to six months of the year in Florida, but want to remain members of St. John-by-the-Gas-Station in Minneapolis or Elyria. Under the following rubrics they can become members of the Churches in Florida:

> *Constituent Members:* people who are ministered to in some sacred act or in counseling, or in special need.
>
> *Affiliate Members:* people of the same denomination from a congregation elsewhere, who want to remain on the membership roll of that congregation.
>
> *Associate Members:* people of another denomination who likewise want to remain on their original congregation's membership list.

The advantage of setting up these categories is that the pastor can minister to these people. In some cases, these special members are allowed to take office and do everything that other members can do. But the arrangement allows them to remain a member "back home."

A cynical reading of the unchurchedness of a sun-belt community like Sarasota might suggest that people had formerly been members of churches for reasons less than spiritual. The analyst is tempted to think that they chose the Church in their younger years up North because it was a part of business life, or because they wanted to be better known or to win a place in the community's power structure. Are more people than we know part of the Christian churches for illegitimate reasons? Is what we are seeing in Florida the real thing, and not the artificial? Yet it might be too harsh to call many of the people unchurched in their new retirement home. Many will be able to answer with a rejoinder, "But I heard a sermon today, I saw the Mass or the crusade on TV, I sent my contribution last week, my prayer request was even on the air the other day."

One of the ministers talked about using the church as a way station, not unlike the hostels set up by friars of old to give hospitality to travelers. He described the element that comes to Florida with all kinds of dreams, and instead finds a lot of brokenness:

> The unfortunate thing is they will always be traveling from place to place because Florida is not the land of dreams, Florida is not swaying palm trees, it is not beaches. It's a place where money is just as valued as any place else. Where a skill is marketable, non-skill and dreams are not. And the cost of living is just as high if not higher than anywhere else. People are just as hard and callous down here, because we are a composite of all the hard and callous people who came from up North, escaping from northern problems, trying to escape down here. It's not a friendly, lovable place. It's tough at times. Because of this, I think people are disenchanted, disoriented, hurting. And it's hard sometimes to find a church when that pain is going on.

Yet some remarkable ministries have been set up to reach out, to draw in, to form Christian community. Probably the fastest growing church in the county, in terms of numbers, is The Tabernacle. The "Tab" follows in the train of those large, independent congregations of evangelical persuasion that have shown up in other counties. Their recent billboard campaign pictured a knotted length of rope. "Jesus Unties the Knots" was the caption. In response to a telephone number on the billboard, over 30,000 phone calls were received. Many left their name and number after the devotional message stopped. There was a follow-up on these respondents.

The Pastor of the Tabernacle, Neville Gritt, and his staff are filling the sanctuary with happy and inspired people. They are also engaged in a Christian school program, a remarkable ministry for and by youth operating in the youth building, the Carpenter's Shop, separated by miles from the main auditorium. Future plans call for the construction of missionary housing, retirement facilities and a needed expansion of their own building. With parties for "single saints" and a Christmas Eve service to be held twice in the city's large Van Wezel Performing Arts Hall, The Tabernacle is gaining increased visibility. Its staff and lay leaders seem ready to work cooperatively with fellow religious leaders and to share some of the things that seem to be working for them.

Other individual congregations also stand out among those I visited: St. Boniface Episcopal and Sarasota's downtown Redeemer Episcopal Churches showed vitality under spirited leadership. St. Martha's Catholic Church in Sarasota and Epiphany in Venice expressed a warm feeling of cooperation. They were both ministering to increasingly large congregations. Beneva Christian, Concordia and Nokomis Lutheran, Trinity and Venice-Nokomis United Methodist congregations could easily give the names of some former unchurched who are now members of their fellowships. Several of the black pastors expressed an enthusiasm and optimism about their ministries. The Presbyterian Church of the Covenant stood out as a congregation offering varied programs on the edge of southern Sarasota city, in a rapidly growing area.

Many of the outstanding clerical leaders in this county would be impressive in just about any metropolitan area. I felt that here, with a surging new migration, the Church is in good hands. Fr. Patrick Clarke of St. Martha's Catholic Church in Sarasota gathered a large inquiry class. I interviewed four members who were willing to stay after the close of the lesson and share their enthusiasm. Pastor Neville Gritt of The Tabernacle introduced me to the large congregation and arranged for formerly unchurched members to be interviewed one after the other in his office.

More people in Sarasota than in the other counties turned to the Church because of "a feeling of emptiness." I found people who admitted that, while so many things seemed to be going well, they sensed a yawning lack of meaning in their lives which led them—along a circuitous route in some cases—to fellowship in a Christian community.

There were some unexpected twists to busy church life. One of the pastors reluctantly gave me a current bulletin when I asked for it. He pointed out that a young, inexperienced person did the secretarial work the past week. With some embarrassment he showed the listing of the second hymn on the worship program: "Just as I am—Without one Flea."

INGHAM COUNTY, MICHIGAN

I chose Ingham County (1975 population 267,581) as a seventh county to add to the original six for several reasons. It reflects the regional concentration of unchurched in the lower peninsula of Michigan, an area that Russell Hale eliminated from consideration as his last cut. Its metropolitan area, Lansing/East Lansing, would help balance the semi-rural nature of four of the other counties. A major university there has its special religious challenge, and campus churches reach out to the unchurched. The denominations are well-represented and well-balanced, almost in proportion to their national strengths. Finally, industry and state government attract large numbers of minority workers.

I got a reverse welcome from a local booster. When the Lutheran Council's Office of Communication and Interpretation sent ahead some material concerning my arrival to help give me better visibility via radio and TV, one Lansing station reacted in an unexpected way. It broadcast a television editorial in which a prominent citizen defended Ingham County against the charge that it was a "highly unchurched area in the Midwest." Pointing

out the existence of 261 local churches, he concluded, "Churches
don't build themselves, they are built by their congregations."
The editorial ended with the comment, "We think spiritual values
in Ingham County have been erroneously misjudged." As is often
the case in situations like this, the negative publicity provoked
heightened interest in my project.

Well, what do the statistics show? Of the nearly 70 counties in
the lower peninsula, more than half show 50 to 70 percent of their
population with no church affiliation. That is a different picture
from neighboring Ohio and Indiana. It is almost as if someone
wrote a different scenario for the religious history of Michigan.
In *Churches and Church Membership 1971*, Ingham County is
listed as having 150 churches. Their total membership equals just
less than 40 percent of the county's population. While the edi-
torialist was defending "our hometown folks" from being "classified in such a manner," the nagging question remained, "Why did
this county and its neighbors show a higher percentage of unchurched than many other counties?" And of course, my more
pressing concern was, "Are there people joining the churches in
Ingham, people who had been unchurched?"

Michigan is the seventh most populous state, counting almost
nine million citizens, quite a growth from the 4,762 who lived
within its borders when the Michigan territory was defined in
1810. With the influx of foreign-born people around the turn of
this century, it has become a collage of diverse races and cultures.

Professor Fred Graham, of the religion department at Michigan
State University, theorized about why the lower peninsula
should be so highly unchurched:

Being churched is highly correlated with being part of a community. And I have a theory. It's only a theory; it would take
a historian to check it out. My theory is that migrating peoples who came to Michigan—with the exception of the Dutch—
did not come as communities, but came as isolates. In my
own family history, whenever these Scotch-Irish people came
west, there were Grahams. When one of them went into Michigan, they just disappeared. Chances are that they disappeared
from church as well. You do not have groups migrating into

Michigan and settling as they did in other parts of the Midwest.

Within Ingham County, the Catholics today number about 40,000 or 15 percent of the population. Methodists are second, with 15,000 or 6 percent.

The MSU campus is surrounded by striking church buildings which represent just about every major denomination. The Christian Reformed Church has printed on its bulletin words that reflect the prevailing opinion among the campus pastors, "We also provide an open and helpful context in which questions may be raised so that the process of making the Faith real and significant in a difficult age may take place."

St. John's Student Parish ministers to an estimated 8,000 Catholics on campus. About half that number attend the several Masses offered every week. "We're not so much a community on Sunday; we are an assembly of communities," said Fr. Jake Foglio, an outstanding Catholic priest. The parish serves university faculty and staff and townspeople as well as students. There are a variety of sub-groups in the parish such as couples who have been on Marriage Encounter, a charismatic community, catechists, those who have made a "Cursillo" (a spiritual retreat weekend), a group that follows the "Ashes to Easter" program, and others.

Professor Graham sees a renewed interest in religion courses in the last ten years. He recalled:

The so-called Jesus movement of the late 1960s and early 70s did to a great extent come out of a milieu out West of people who had indeed tried everything and found nothing worked. I've seen many a student on our campus now part of a prayer group or a Bible study group—whose older brothers and sisters were my students and who were into drugs. I think there was a great deal of experimentation that didn't work out very well in human life. Also the answers to the complex problems in our society are so difficult to imagine. They're not simple like we once thought they were: throw a few rocks through the student union, smoke a little grass, and bring down President Johnson. There's certainly a sense in which the student population is much more religious now. A lot of that, I'm convinced, is because other things didn't work, and perhaps this will. I would like to think that indeed it does work—they find their lives healthier, happier, fuller.

In addition, the "rooting" process that takes place when young people start their own families leads them to investigate anew the Church's claims, Graham pointed out.

An evangelism-centered congregation is situated south of Lansing, far from the university campus in the suburb of Holt. This church, St. Matthew Lutheran, has a remarkable track record. It has grown from 450 to 1800 baptized members, making it the "fastest growing Lutheran church in the Missouri Synod." According to the minister of evangelism, "About 90 percent of us are converts to Christianity in the last nine years. We came from 27 different denominational backgrounds. Today, by the grace of God, we are Christian Lutherans and loving every moment of it. Over 600 of us adults have trained in this evangelism method (or, as we call it, the 'Pass it on' program) over the past few years." He continued, "Those who were brought in through the witnessing program say, 'If someone didn't take enough time to come and visit me, I would still be on my way to hell. So for the fact that you took time out of your busy schedule to do this and saw it as a top priority mission, I hold it as a top priority in my life too.' So many people have joined the witnessing program for that fact."

With regard to evangelism, one of the Episcopal ministers said of his campus parish, "The community that I'm part of here, which would be the Episcopal ministry at MSU, is a solidly sacramental, Biblically-centered, liturgically-centered worshiping community." Contacting students by letter, he announced that he would be in a small room near the church entrance during certain hours of the day. "My strategy," he said, "was availability—let them know that I'm available to them." He also commented on why so many members of the Church fall away when they go to the university:

I feel it is left pretty much up to every individual person to chart his or her relationship with the Church. And a good many of the acolytes would come to church only when they were responsible for serving. Well, I knew immediately that that was not going to sustain anything. I feel there is a way that you can communicate to people and teach them and help them understand the relationship between Faith and the institutional Church—and I think that can be done.

Another Lutheran congregation, Ascension, on the east side, conducts an annual art fair. The church itself bought several of the pieces. The narthex has some dazzling examples of painting, weaving, sculpture with metal can-ends and collage. Pastor Roy Schroeder's ministry to the art community is well received.

Asked what is the most common problem people who are leaving the Church have, Fr. Jake Foglio of St. John's answered:

I think it's non-relevance. I don't think what we said is preparing for the program today. The people don't have great reasons for bolting—they just go out the back door. The Church seems irrelevant to their lives at some point. They have no reason for continued membership or continued activity. That's a combination of apathy and lack of knowledge of what it's about. It no longer fits their lifestyle. But a lot of people bounce back when they start "rooting."

I asked him what bridges he could build to the unchurched, that non-community. "Credibility," he said. "You have to be credible. They find out that at St. John's there are welcoming people. They feel comfortable here and then they say 'I re-found Christ.' Some people come here to keep warm, some people come because Christ is a 'nice person. . . .' An invitation to the unchurched might be for a wedding here, a funeral, seeing someone get help in counseling. They find out that this might be OK. And they feel the need for community and check it out."

While a majority of Ingham County residents might still prefer not to check out the Church, I found a vitality, an inviting warmth, and a desire to reach out on the part of many parishes, particularly those around the university. And just the Saturday before I arrived, a staff writer for the *State Journal* wrote under the headline, "Churches Cement Community Ties," "New in the area? Greater Lansing's more than 250 churches and synagogues, embracing more than 60 denominations and all major faiths, offer one of the most promising and fastest ways to make friends and to get involved. They also offer, perhaps more than other organizations, an opportunity for family togetherness, through worship and other religiously-oriented programs." It was the first time in many years I'd seen something like "togetherness" in print. Yet a number of people whom I interviewed agreed with those comments and might have been seeking just that.

3

Why the People Who Came Back
Dropped Out in the First Place

Before asking why the formerly unchurched returned to the fold, we need to glance at their reasons for leaving. Hale's *Who Are the Unchurched?* approaches this question from a broad perspective. Our task is simpler, to see the "dropping out" specifically from the viewpoint of people who came back. Was their experience, in the words of Halford E. Luccock, a "lovers' quarrel with the Church"? Did they never leave in their heart of hearts? Or was it a real death and resurrection? A cutting of the cord of faith only to tie it up again in a new life? For some, was it a turning their back on God and the Church until a complex of events spun them around, or until they "came to themselves"? Or could we say that God never breaks His covenant, even though human beings may temporarily break theirs? As one Episcopalian woman said of her return to the Church after many years, "It came to me that my Baptism was a valid commitment."

Let the formerly unchurched speak for themselves. They gave various answers to the questions, "What was your religious background?" or "Why did you drop out of the Church?" Some told of childhood church contacts that included daily Mass, attendance at parochial school, or awards for regular involvement in Sunday School. Others indicated a more occasional commitment. Some people admitted that they had had no contact with any church at all as a child. George Gallup, in his analysis of unchurched Americans, states that the percentage of respondents who reported no childhood religious training rose from 9 percent a decade ago to 17 percent in 1978. In some cases, people whom I interviewed faulted their parents for pushing or demanding attendance. Others remember that their parents gave them only perfunctory encouragement and blamed their own lack of interest on this.

I urged the respondents to think back to that time of dropping their ties with the Church. They recalled different reasons for their disengagement and their decision to walk alone.

Jane mentioned that she had been baptized a Lutheran and then went to the local Methodist church as a child "with all my friends. That's where I attended most of my childhood." But then the pattern broke down. She blamed it on the lack of encouragement from her family. "I stopped going probably in the eighth grade. None of them [her family] wanted to go. So I just kind of lost interest. When you're the only one and trying to go all by yourself, it's not an easy thing to do." Daniel, now living in Monmouth, Oregon, remembers growing up in a little Lutheran town near a Catholic community. "We didn't go to church. And that, you know, is hard for me to explain. I think my folks were Christian people; I believe that. But they just didn't go to church. As a result, us kids really didn't."

When a churched person marries someone who has no religious background, that can become an occasion for both to avoid church involvement. Nina, for example, recalled for me her membership in different Protestant Churches as a young person, including regular Sunday and Wednesday worship and Bible study. Her marriage to someone with no church affiliation made it tempting for her to drop out of her Church. "I basically did not go to church for, oh five or six years," she said.

Some interviewees recalled that they attended congregations of several denominations. This was due to moving around or to following friends and neighbors or to an indifference on the part of parents, perhaps because of mixed religious loyalty. Lee, a 45-year-old farmer, now an active leader in his congregation in Oregon, said, "I went to church with my parents kind of intermittently. We weren't, I would say, regular Presbyterians. Plus a variety of Sunday Schools, Baptist and Presbyterian."

Fred, a 25-year-old in Holt, Michigan, blamed the confusion about religion in his family on the mixed background of his parents. He remembers his early religious training as "very, very sketchy for the most part. Atheistic as far as my father's concerned. My mother was Baptist when she was young. Definite conflict there. Kids went to church, to Sunday School, once in a while."

Some young people remember a deep religious experience that didn't stick. Roy, a factory worker in his thirties who lives near Dallas, Oregon, recalled, "When I was in the seventh grade I went over to Newport, and I went on a church retreat with my cousin. I remember going up to the church and the altar, and I really felt my first coming to the Lord. From then until three years ago, I lost all touch. Neither my mom or dad goes to church; they never have." I asked Roy if he considered himself a Christian during those years when he was outside the Church, particularly after he had answered the altar call. "At the time," he replied, "I don't think I really knew what it was. At that time I felt it, but when I got back home and wasn't around it, and none of my friends were attending church regularly, it was gone." Carlton, now in the Church of God in Guin, Alabama, claimed a deep religious experience at an early age. "I could feel a tremendous change inside. But as I got older, my attention drew away from religious things because they seemed so gray and dull."

Some interviewees had been urged by parents to go to church and rebelled when they were old enough to get away with it. Myron's comments are typical of a large number of these. "My mom and dad went quite a bit. They got me to go to church; I really didn't want to go. It was there, available. I went until I was considered old enough to make the decision myself, and I decided not to go. About seventh grade I stopped going on my own; and then I just went occasionally when friends of mine went. In high school I went a few times. After high school I just stopped, until just a few years ago." Asked how he felt about the Church during those years, Myron answered, "I really didn't understand anything that was going on. I went because there were people there that I liked. I was very nervous when I was there. I had other things I'd rather do, so I just did them. So things tied my Sundays up." Now a faithful Baptist in Polk County, Oregon, Myron described a history that reveals no strong feelings one way or another. Friends could invite him to attend with them, but there was no initiative from within and no strong encouragement externally. It was simple to drop away.

The people I have mentioned so far slipped out the back door of the Churches. Their attachment was minimal and their falling away apparently produced no big sparks, no guilt feelings in them, no reaction in their congregations. But others left the Churches more consciously and intentionally. Theirs was a rejection, not just a falling away. They made a decision to drop out. For some of them the Church had failed; they had to leave.

Ruth, now a Lutheran in Lansing, Michigan, remembers being a fairly regular member of the Episcopal Church as a young person. But the old rector left, she said, and "The new one was kind of a fire and brimstone type that had just come from a 20-year mission in South America. We just couldn't relate to him. Began finding excuses why we didn't want to go to church and just kind of drifted off."

Grayson spoke for many who remember their teen-age rebellion and its effect on church life. He resented people "taking over" for him, he explained:

I think young people—my age bracket [25]—were brought up with "go to school, you hafta do this by this rule, do that by that rule." All during your beginning years, adolescence and up until you're an adult, you have someone tell you what to do. It's always a "take-over" deal. Young people look at church sort of like it's "take-over"—and that's what they're trying to get away from. And I notice in a lot of Churches today they're getting toward a more relaxed atmosphere, kinda make it a point to stress that they're an informal Church. Those Churches are growing by leaps and bounds. People are looking. I know if I were looking for a Church, I'd look for a Church where I could feel comfortable.

Grayson feels that the Church of God of Prophecy in Marion County fills that requirement. Harold complained about the Church's unwillingness to keep up with the times. "I belonged to the Church in 1960. And it's the same now as it was then. I said to my wife, 'You could look at the bulletin, just change the date, and you'd have the 1960's bulletin.' I think that's horrible, because you're in a changing society." Bonnie looked back upon her feelings when she was unchurched. She resented the strong, zealous evangelism aimed at her. "I remember what it was like, being an atheist and being chased by Jesus freaks on the subways of New York. I don't believe in it."

Just the act of moving damaged some tender religious roots. Without all the former support systems, the relationship to church does not easily transplant. Barry, a member now of the Japanese Free Methodist Church in Anaheim, California, mentioned that he dropped out of church through "moving away from home and church, losing contact. It gets to the point where you get detached from your old group. You used to do certain things like going to church and things like that, and when you get detached or you move away you meet new friends, and if their background was not church-going, then you tend to blend in with it, and I think that's the way we got kind of lost."

After moving from their Maine home to Connecticut, Dale and Jeannine did not reaffiliate with a Church. "Everything was new to us, and we didn't really get to know that many people who were involved in a Church. And of course we didn't take it on ourselves to go out. We didn't talk about it. It wasn't a topic at the time." After marriage Jane and her husband moved to Dallas, Oregon and didn't attend any church for five years. "We didn't know anyone who was a Lutheran and we didn't take the initiative to go and find out, and it was just easier to sleep in on Sunday mornings. Then after we went to church, we found there were quite a few people we had seen around, and we had sort of known, and we had no idea that they were members of the Church."

Variations on the theme of hypocrisy were given as reasons for turning away from the Church. Hal said of the church of his youth in Alabama, "I was in the Church, but I didn't see any difference in the big people in the Church. They'd have an argument over who'd teach three people in Sunday School. It turned me off." Claims that people did one thing on Sunday and something very different the rest of the week were made by others to justify their exit from the Churches.

The Church itself was faulted by some interviewees. For example, Veronica, now a Methodist, accused her former Church of overlooking her spiritual needs. "I thought a lot of times that church people, if they see somebody floundering away, should go, right then, don't wait, and say, 'Can I help you? Have you got this problem? We miss you, we need you.' And we fail to do this. And I felt at times that the Church let me down when maybe I needed that encouragement." Bob, remembering his youth in New England before moving to Oregon, said, "I belonged to the youth fellowship in the Congregational Church, and pretty much was involved in it, even though no one had ever—I never got the idea of salvation. This is what I realized later on in life—that it never happened." Speaking of his Methodist family, Stan said, "My father was disappointed in some things that happened in his church. Thus I kind of got a little negative toward church for quite a while. So from my high school to my junior year in college, I really didn't know Christ in any way, or didn't recognize Him— that's a better way of putting it."

Some complained that there was no fellowship, no spirit of community in the Church as they remember it. Jim and his family went to a Protestant church in Lansing, Michigan and they had the children baptized there. Soon they fell away from that congregation. Jim commented, "We found really no commitment there at all. Nothing drew us to stay, and we used the excuse for a long time that we could do our praying at home, we could do our reading at home, which was nothing but a cop out." Although she had gone to parochial school and belonged to Catholic youth groups, May, another drop-out, said, "I had not had any kind of rewarding Christian experience with other people. I didn't find the spiritual food, or whatever, in the worship that was happening in that parish on Sundays." After 12 years outside of the Church, May rejoined via the St. John's Student Parish at Michigan State University.

When Walter returned from military service to his home church in Logan, West Virginia he felt that people didn't want him back. "There were people standing there that I knew—this was before the service started. And no one had still said anything to me, shook hands with me or anything. I got the feeling that thoughts were, 'What's he doing here? He doesn't belong here.' I just went outside. I waited in the car for my grandmother till the service was over. I never did go back anymore."

Sleep took over Sunday for people who were working long hours during the rest of the week. Craig recalled that work pressures were a real hindrance to regular worship life. "When I was in Flint Junior College," he asserted, "then I worked my way through, and Sunday mornings I usually slept in. That was the day I could, rather than go to church." Nora had a variation on that. "It was just laziness and not wanting to be involved."

Many young people, when asked, claimed that they felt no need for the Church during their years of absence from worship services. For example, Rodger, a landscape architect who lives near Monmouth, Oregon, remembers attending Presbyterian Sunday School as a youngster. "But then I sort of turned away, didn't really even think about it." He claimed that he didn't think of himself as a Christian while away from the Church. Only after marrying a practicing Lutheran did Rodger seriously think about his own relationship to a church. Tom, now active again in the Catholic Church, remembers that at about the age of eighteen, "It struck me that going to church wasn't necessarily making me a better person, so I gradually weaned myself away from active participation."

An exceptional case would be the New York physician who went to Sunday School at five, and began asking himself a year later why he was going. "I got into a questioning at age six, whether I actually believed that there did exist such an entity [as God]. I decided 'no.' So that was the last time I went to church for the next 20 years."

Vera, who was raised Catholic, went to a Protestant college and found few Catholic friends. She recalled, "I didn't feel that I meant anything to the Church. I didn't feel that I needed religion either, at that time. There were just too many other things that I was concerned with." Dorene went to Baptist Sunday School. Later, she said, "I went to college and quit going to church and kind of rejected everything I'd ever been taught. Just kind of figured, 'Some people need that, I don't. I can be cool without it. I don't know if there's a God or not, but if there is, I don't think He's concerned about me.' And I just did my own thing."

Doctrinal conflict emerged as a reason for leaving for people who rejected what the Church taught or misunderstood its message. Sherry, a Californian, explained her falling away from her Church as the result of not listening carefully to what was being taught. Asked if she felt that she was a Christian while outside of the Church, she answered:

Yes. I felt that I was a very moral person. I worked in a birth defects clinic for two years and believed that I found my God in other people. I guess I had not come to terms with my religion yet. I don't know that I still have. I'm working on it. I'm growing in it. But at that point it was not an adult way of viewing religion. I had never grown up from the little child who thought of a God in heaven. And I had had just enough training where I didn't know if it was right or not to think of not believing in a God in heaven. I really didn't know because I never questioned it in college, and after that I never had intimate contact with anyone in religion to discuss it with.

Halford, a long time resident of Independence, Oregon, compared his early admiration for the Farmer's Union in North Dakota and their concern for the "welfare of all people" with the different emphasis he found in the Churches. "I had a lot of concern for people and there was always this conflict in me of why the religious people couldn't have these concerns, or more of them couldn't, like I had. Real religious people that I didn't question at all seemed to be concerned with the dead and dying Christ and salvation. I felt that any God that I could follow had to be concerned about life here on earth and people's relations to one another."

Avoiding a God of law and judgment was the reason given by some who left their Church. Said Veronica, "For a long time, I really had this picture of God sitting up there and saying 'Hold on—you dare not make a mistake!' "

Church membership was a casualty when in times of tragedy people blamed God. Mack, 35, a sporting goods department manager, admitted that he held a grudge against God for many years. He had been a member of a non-denominational congregation in Lansing, Michigan:

> I did have a wonderful encounter in the Sunday School when I was younger. I got some groundwork. But basically I rejected the Church, especially after my father's death. It was a long, lingering type of death, and I prayed for death, and for different things. And I just said, 'Lord, you're not there.' And then I took along with it the Church, decided it was a moneymaking institution and really did not have any value to people in itself, because I did not see any help given me or my family.

Bob, in Cypress, California, said that his father's sudden and agonizing death sent the family into a painful crisis and caused a retreat from the Church. "We were at the hospital when it happened," Bob recalled:

> My brother just went straight outside the main doors there and looked up. Using some foul language, he said, speaking to God, "If you're there . . . you really blew it, and you're a no-good, worthless . . ." And that was it. I went all to hell in a handbasket. And I found it too hard for a long time to get my faith back. My mom couldn't handle all this and she became an alcoholic—though she had not been a drinker. And

then we had children—my daughter was born about a year after my dad's passing. And finally I had to take and rationalize things in my own mind and give credit where credit was due. If God had taken my father, then I equally had to give Him credit for giving us our daughter. You had to balance the books there somehow. Of course I prayed very hard and it didn't pan out. And that's pretty hard to swallow when you've been taught through Sunday School, "Knock and the door will open, ask and ye shall receive." I was down on my hands and knees in the backyard, and he just flat died. Then I matured some, started realizing that the trees grow and die, plants grow and die. We grow and, as mortal earthlings, we pass away. I believe very strongly that that isn't the end. So I guess the strongest tie to bring me back in was the children. I don't know, if we hadn't any children, where I'd be right now as far as going to church.

Church was described as gray and dull by some interviewees who tried to recapture what their feelings were when they dropped out of membership and attendance. Louise, now living in Belfast, Maine, talked about her early religious training and how, after marriage, she fell away from the Church. "It just seemed boring to me, to just sit there for an hour. And yet, I'm not knocking my background, because I received great faith from it. I was 22 years of age. I started saying that I was not going for an hour a week. I knew that there must be more." Martha recalled attending the Lutheran Church regularly with her family after the confirmation of her oldest daughter. But her son left that Church. "One Sunday my son got up—he was a sophomore—and he just went home in tears from church. It was kind of the same routine over and over. He was a terribly sincere young guy. He said, 'I just feel like I'm dying, sitting there.' A really sad experience for him." They found in one of the Mennonite congregations in Dallas, Oregon "in-depth Bible study . . . with lots of things going on for the kids."

People dropped out of church for various reasons. Common experiences are an erosion of interest, filling up the gaps with other things, rebelling against parental urging or, in the opposite case, becoming apathetic because of parental disinterest.[1] Young people followed friends to different churches, then began to follow friends who belonged to no church. Some began testing the waters outside of church life, and found them pleasant. Some said they left the Church because it demanded too much; a few complained that it demanded too little. Through the tinted glasses of those moving out, the Church and things religious "seemed so gray and dull." Life looked more colorful in the "far country."

---

1. Dean R. Hoge and David A. Roozen, in *Understanding Church Growth and Decline: 1950-1978* (New York: Pilgrim Press, 1979), offer valuable research insights into factors influencing church commitment.

4

Why People Join the Church

The question, "Why do the unchurched join the Church?" is answered here in the words of 180 people who were unchurched for several years but have now joined a Church. The significance of these answers lies not in numbers but in the testimony of people as to what changed their lives.

Some give their answers in a simple, clear way. Others pause and struggle over their description of events that they may not have analysed before. A few speak passionately, even eloquently, about what happened to them along a spiritual journey. An outsider to their experience might suggest that their return to the Church reflects the accident of timing, the power of human persuasion, or the gullibility of people confronted by a dynamic preacher or by zealous church members. While acknowledging the human side of it, some new church members feel forced to point out that God was active in themselves and others to bring about His will.

When an interview seemed to be headed for a dead end, I cut it short after just a few minutes. Some people just weren't able to

61

articulate a coherent story. When confronting a new Methodist recently arrived from Korea, I found myself struggling so much over the linguistic hurdles that I abandoned the effort. Also, a few very old people tended to drift into other streams of thought. On the other hand, some interviews extended beyond the one-hour limit of the tape. A few people spoke of problems in their congregations, or with their minister, and it seemed more appropriate to talk about these matters in private conversation, with the tape recorder off. For example, after a luncheon radio interview in Maine, one of the radio announcers in the studio phoned me at the restaurant. We spent over an hour together at the station in pastoral conversation about some church problems his family was having. But these are exceptions; for the most part the interviews followed clearly defined goals.

Humor often punctuated an otherwise deeply moving story. I will try to share some of those lighter moments. Such humor served both as a break in an otherwise intense recollection and also as an appropriate response to the absurdity of God working in mysterious ways with His wayward children. Perhaps it was one of God's wry jokes to send a carpenter as an unanticipated evangelical witness to an unchurched family struck by debilitating illness. One interviewee saw it that way. Another related how his family was involved in so many activities in their new Catholic parish. He ended with, "We're Catholic as hell now," and laughed.

The key question in the interview was something like this, "What made you think of joining a Church at this time?" It was rephrased as one of the closing questions. "Of all the different things that happened to you in your life, what main thing led you to the Church at this time?" Often my respondents paused a while before they answered. The two questions were sort of a check on each other, but I found that although the answers were usually alike, some people explained them differently.

People of different denominations at times answered in very similar phrases and words. On occasion, I thought I heard echoes from the pastor's sermons or repeated emphases in one congregation's life in the responses from different members of the same church. And yet the individuals cast their net out for those religious truths that fit their needs at a particular time.

Some responses were more common in one region than another. In West Virginia and Alabama people were more at ease using "God talk" and often expressed their religious convictions in terms of getting on the right road to heaven. People in Oregon more often spoke of the loving fellowship of a congregation that drew them in, or referred to the influence of good friends or neighbors. The sophisticated college students that attended worship services in student centers around Michigan State University spoke more intellectually about their faith experience than did people who lived in rural areas. Not surprisingly, rural and small town people often described their entrance into the Churches in terms of family concerns and pressures.

Following are the categories of reasons that people gave for joining a Church. They speak of internal pressures and external influences. Some interviewees shifted gears midway in their story to indicate more than one reason for their decision. Just a very few admitted they "didn't know" why they joined.

THE INFLUENCE OF CHRISTIAN PEOPLE

Christian people, intentionally or casually or without even realizing it, were a force drawing people to the Churches. Their witness was made by silent example or by verbal testimony. Twenty-two interviewees said that they saw a difference in the quality of life of a friend, relative, neighbor or co-worker, and they connected that difference in some way to the person's religious conviction or church membership. Thus unchurched individuals received a message that caused them to ask questions about their own lifestyle and to seek answers from the person that prompted this questioning. Others were persuaded—sometimes pestered—by church members who urged them to change their ways. The settings ranged from car pools to bars to kitchen tables to a chemistry lab.

One respondent noted that Christians are "being observed." Their actions, even attitudes, make an impression on people around them. Their poise under stress, their unreasonable happiness, even the small favors they do without thinking—these are elements that make a silent witness powerful. A new member of the Free Will Baptist Church in Guin, Alabama said, "I could see people—Christians—handling situations that I wouldn't know how to handle. And I could see them take this situation and work it out, whether it be a money situation, or sickness or a death. I could see them handling that situation. I knew then that there was something great there that a person ought to find."

In the same vein, a dockworker from Searsport, Maine recalled, "My best friend started going [to church] before I did, you know. And I watched him. I knew he wouldn't lie to me. But still I thought he was crazy because he was going to church all the time. . . ." "Specially on New Year's Eve," his wife added. Bill continued, "He stopped in here every night. If you want to get somebody involved in the Church, I think the best thing to do, the only thing you can do better than talking, is—the people are watching you. Your actions count more than your words do. If you're living what you're telling, that's all right. But if you're not, you'll never get anybody to go." When I asked, "Did you see something different in your friend's life?," he replied, "Oh yeah. Gee, oh yeah. He just quit drinking, not that he was trying to, but it was just his whole lifestyle changed. Just like overnight. From going to dances with us, to going to church. . . ."

It was somewhat surprising to hear of people choosing churches on the basis of friendship or even the advice of acquaintances. Perhaps this speaks of a lack of deep religious or traditional roots. The straight road of denominational loyalty that has kept so many of us in the same religious environment has for others been washed away. Excessive moving, disappointment with a congregation, intellectual disdain for dogma, or a poor religious education have made it easy for some to wander out of a traditional path. They are free to pick and choose (or not choose) until someone else reveals a quality of life, a firm conviction, an ability to cope—or just says a concerned word or two. If the ensuing church visit is satisfying, the formerly unchurched person may be on his or her way to a well-founded membership.

Merrill, a young Oregon lab technician, talked about influencing others by example:

> I want my actions to tell a lot of the story. And a lot of people at work realize right off that I'm different from some people. It doesn't take very long for someone to recognize that, "Hey, he doesn't use foul language, he doesn't cuss when he hits his finger with a hammer. He may get upset, but he calms down pretty quickly." Someone asked me once, "Don't you really get upset, really mad?" Yeah, I have. Then I start smiling; it works. Then they may start asking "Why?" Then some get quiet. I used to get quiet. I know what that felt like.

Former Episcopalians now living in Fountain Valley, California talked of their conversion, "It was a combination of many things. But a lot of it had to do with some people we met who happened to be Catholics. But that had nothing to do with it, either, because they never proselytized us or anything. It was just their unmistakable love for us. . . ."

When Christians make their witness verbal, it is strengthened if their lifestyle corresponds closely to their words. But the verbal witness has its own focus. Relatives, friends, or even chance acquaintances seek to share the Faith and the Church. The event is not organized like evangelism; it often happens in an unplanned, spontaneous—some would say accidental—way.

A young man from a non-practicing Jewish family in Maine went to college on the West Coast. He recalled:

> I met this girl who was a Methodist. The first time we went out, she just started talking. We went over to some place where she was living, and two of her girfriends—one's a Baptist and the other one was Methodist—played their guitars and stuff. And they played religious-type music. We ended up talking that evening. . . . And she really got me thinking because she was pretty religious. And I guess I just kept on reading and reading. And she gave me a Bible. I borrowed it from her and read that. I really couldn't understand things. I remember I was really having problems—this was a few months later—and I went to the ocean for a weekend. I just read a Bible all that weekend, the New Testament. That's when I

really came to understand I really did believe in Christ. And I knew that He was real ... and I brought other people into the Faith, which has been the greatest feeling I ever had in my life. And I joined a [Methodist] church. I got baptized, and when I got baptized, it was really significant.

Dan, a community leader in Monmouth, Oregon from an unchurched home, looked back and said, "I don't know why I didn't go [to church], except it just wasn't part of the life I knew when I was growing up. I really didn't go to church until a man that I knew and for whom I had a great deal of admiration and respect, our next door neighbor, kept talking to me about the Church. He is the man that I really credit with getting me into the church here." When his friend told him that the little Lutheran congregation was going to build a new church, he answered:

If you ever build a church, I'll go sit in the front row of that thing when you first open it up. And I kept my word, except that the church was full and I couln't sit in the front row. I had to sit in the back row. I don't know really why I did that except that it was out of respect for Lyle more than anything. And that might sound a little bit funny, but he's a man that I felt had real strong Christian beliefs. I really listened to Lyle and learned a tremendous amount from him.

Evelyn, a member of the Catholic charismatic group at Michigan State University's St. John Student Parish, remembers the Christian people who influenced her:

I got in a little bit of trouble and got kicked out of my apartment, and it was the middle of the year, and I needed to find another place to live. And I was talking with this one friend of mine and telling her about it—this is the one who kept trying to get me to go to church. And she said, "Well, I'll pray for you, pray that God will help." I said, "Mary, what good's that going to do?" She said, "Well, you'll be surprised." I said, "Well look, you go ahead and pray; I don't think it'll do any good, but it can't hurt." And the next day Mary came to me, and she said, "Evelyn, I've got a place for you to live." It was true, she did. And it was a good location, it was just what I wanted. It also meant living with four other Christian girls, but it was right about then that I decided maybe that's what I needed too. Because I'd seen something happening.... It didn't seem to be a game anymore. Like Mary had a relationship with Somebody, and when she prayed, something happened. I guess that was one of the barriers that I put up that started coming down.

She first went to a Presbyterian Church, then returned home after graduation and attended the Baptist Church there. On a weekend campout, Evelyn met another girl who, she says, "really had an impact on my life." Evelyn added:

And she started telling me about those prayer meetings that they held over at St. John's [Catholic Church] here in East Lansing. Charismatic prayer meetings—that sounds really weird. But she finally talked me into going, and that was probably the biggest change, because I went to one. And here are all these people talking in some language, and praising the Lord. And all the time that I've grown up, you prayed one at a time out loud—you took turns praying. I wasn't unfamiliar with praying out loud. I was a bit unfamiliar with everybody at once praying out loud, but they praised God. And that was foreign to me. But I saw a lot of love from the people there and met a few of the people. Tremendous capacity for love. And so I kept going back.

Jim, a fireman in Lansing of Methodist upbringing, was married in his Church, but his wife had no religious background. Their children got to playing with children down the street, which brought together the two wives, then the two families, and they became close friends. The other family was Catholic and went to Mass regularly, but did not seem "involved in the community in the church." The two couples went to parties together, and "the friend thing was going great," according to Jim. "And then they made a Cursillo [spiritual retreat]. Both of them attended Cursillo weekends. And we noticed a change in them. It was quite a drastic change." When the parish had its first campout, Jim recalled, he and his wife "hemmed and hawed around and tried to think up excuses not to go." He continued, "But we said, 'Well, all these people we've been going to parties and dances and having fun with are going to be there.' So we went. Thoroughly enjoyed it, just the community and the togetherness, and we went to Mass that night. Outdoor Mass."

An inquiry class began a few weeks later. A friend invited them to attend. "Well, I was interested and I guess at the time we'd say that we were both searching. We had a void in our lives that we didn't realize at the time. And maybe that's just a little push that we needed." The following February Jim made a retreat. "I guess that's really where I got myself straightened out," he said. "I had time to spend with myself and really meditate and think about my life—where I was going, what I'd done, and how I'd wasted a portion of my life. We were really excited about belonging to the Church and thoroughly enjoyed going to Mass. We still do." A later experience with Cursillo and the group reunions that follow have made religion a very solid foundation for this family's life together.

A girlfriend invites the boy to church for a social evening. A friend constantly urges a former church member to attend church with him. Brother goes to youth camp and returns with news—he's accepted the Lord. An acquaintance at a bar invites two young men to a potluck sponsored by his church. At her 41st birthday party, a woman in Sarasota is converted by a friend who just talked quietly with her in a corner of the room during the festivities. These were typical of the stories I heard of unchurched people being influenced by Christian church members.

A unique and moving narrative was given by a new member of the Searsport Full Gospel Church in Maine. Louise remembers turning her back on her earlier religious upbringing. Although she expressed appreciation for the religious background she received, she noted, "I had been unhappy with what I had seen. Just this one person up there, a focal point. I didn't feel any personal communication. I thought that my God, the great God, would have more feeling ... that there would be communication." Lou found herself married, with five children and outside of any Church. Lou's husband began to have breathing difficulties. Barely forty, he was diagnosed as terminally ill. While he was still able to work full-time as a store manager, Lou went to the store at Christmas time and saw a church group come and perform a "living Christmas tree." She remembers saying to her husband, "I want to know what Church cares that much that they would come out—it was thirty below zero—and stand there and sing for three hours."

Although her husband's condition became worse, the couple still did not feel comfortable walking into an unknown church building. Lou recalled:

Once again, I told God, "I don't think you're listening to me. I'm serious. I want that church home." A whole year has gone by, by this time. And still I didn't feel I wanted to go hopping around Churches. I felt that God was going to direct us to that one Church that would be the one for us. We had to have a shower put in downstairs, because my husband could no longer climb the stairs. Wouldn't you know that this carpenter that came was from that [living Christmas tree] church. We just started talking about God and the goodness of God. He had said that my husband is terribly ill, but I didn't seem depressed. I said, "No. We've had tremendous years. God has been good. We've had five children they were all miracles in themselves. I could be sad if it had been rotten. What's to be sad about?"

When the subject got around to church, the carpenter said that it was his church that had put on the "living Christmas tree" at her husband's store. Lou took the whole family to that church in Searsport the next Sunday. "And we just knew that we were home. We walked in the door, and I just poked in, and I said, 'This is it!' " The pastor arranged for them both to work together in the congregation's fledgling parochial school. Lou's husband experienced a remission for a year, but he died the following October. His widow, as she sat with me, reflected, "I believe that we were given an extra year by God, and it enriched all our lives. What really blessed me was the thought, 'Here God sent His Son as a carpenter to save the world. And then He sends a carpenter to my home.' Now that blew my mind. I thought that was dynamite." I thought so too.

A lapsed Lutheran in Cypress, California tells of a neighbor two doors up who was "constantly asking me to come on over to his church." John continued:

He kept after me long enough, and finally I committed myself one day and said, "Well, we'll go with you in the morning." I was sitting around the pool, sipping a scotch. And we went over to the church and really enjoyed it. One of the reasons—I had a kind of guilt feeling in a way. My children were nine and seven years old in 1971, and I wanted them to go to Sunday School. And I just didn't feel right about dumping them off at the door. And I just needed somebody to give me a good pitch. And the neighbor was it. It's like you're going to have a mole removed. You talk about it, and you never do it. And he was finally the push, and so we went. . . .

Paul, a renewed Baptist from an older part of Lansing, says that his attitude toward the Church changed because of a "neighbor, a couple of houses down here. They asked us if we wanted to participate in the neighborhood Bible study." Paul and his wife—who is still unchurched—accepted "more out of politeness." The group of ten shrank to three couples. Paul recalled, "Going through the book of Mark I was influenced by Jesus' life. I'd had some exposure while I was going to Sunday School, but that was at least six years or so ago, something like that. I really didn't deliberate on it. Now I was thinking about it. Anyway, about a year later, I asked Jesus to be my Savior." In this class, the Church wasn't an issue. The host, a man with some Bible college training, invited people from different backgrounds to the neighborhood Bible study in a home.

Having moved all the way from Pawtucket, Rhode Island to Independence, Oregon, Don answered the question, "How did you become associated with the Church?" with these words, "Well, it was a long, long process. When I first moved up here to Oregon, I kept meeting up with Christians, and they came in all different sizes and shapes. I was talking about my different philosophies and stuff like that, and this fellow turned around and looked at me. He said, 'Don, I just got to clear the record here.

I'm a dyed-in-the-wool Christian.' And I didn't know what that meant, still. I didn't know quite what Christianity meant."

Don also described a situation at an art fair in eastern Oregon, where he was examining a display of Christian symbols done in hand-wrought iron. "And so we got to talking, and immediately they started witnessing to me. They came on really, really strong." Don remembers walking with these long-haired Christian young people after lunch that day. They were met on the sidewalk by some "guys with very short haircuts" who saw them and came at them:

> They saw all this long hair, and they came on like "look what we've got here." And we were kind of looking up at them, I remember that. And they were looking for a fight, and the leader of our group walked right up to the one who was talking the most, and he said, "Do you know Jesus Christ?" And it stopped him cold. He said, "These guys are crazy." And he walked away. There's an awful lot of people that witnessed to me numerous times, and I started realizing my need for salvation slowly but surely through all these different people. I don't know wether they belonged to any particular Church or not.

People came under the influence of Christians in various ways: by example, by word, by invitation. Church members often complain that they are not competent to "make calls." Or they resist appeals to witness because they "don't know the Bible too well." Might they be emboldened to fashion their witness around some of the forms mentioned: inviting others to church, sharing what God means to them, or just living in the awareness that "the people are watching you"? Some may be looking for just that glue that holds church people together. A final example is Dick, son of a Protestant clergyman, who recently joined the Catholic Church in Lansing, Michigan. He describes what happened:

> In a sense, I was a rather good kid for a while. I never wanted to smoke pot or anything, do any of the bad stuff. Then I kind of got off track, everybody kept on persuading me, and I was kind of weak all right. For maybe a couple of months, I kind of gave in. But when I met my girlfriend, it reminded me

of how I used to be. I didn't smoke, I drank on occasions. She
was an inspiration herself. And then when she told me she
went to a Catholic Church, I told her I'd go with her. . . . I
saw the beauty behind her . . . it was kind of speaking to me
where the real world was.

FAMILY RELATIONSHIPS AND RESPONSIBILITIES

It has been a truism, believed by pastors and church leaders, that
young people will most likely take a "vacation" from church for
several years, starting in their teens. It begins when the feelings
of rebellion and independence grow strong enough to break away
from family religious practices. The teen-ager might adopt the
role of rebel by rejecting parents' demands that he or she go to
church with them. The break is probably easier in religiously
lukewarm or indifferent households. The Gallup Poll attests to the
fact that those under 30 assert Christian beliefs and attend church
less often than their elders. This age group reports 29 percent
attendance on a Sunday, compared with the national average of 41
percent.[1] But church leaders feel that the vacation will end when
the young person gets married, settles down, has children and begins to think about Baptism and Sunday School for the new generation.

In years past this scenario has been played out often enough to
be credible. The pastor of a Christian Church in Huntington
Beach, California was optimistic. He remarked:

Even though they've had faith in the past, now they're on
vacation from their Faith. But they're reachable. There's
something within them, and the Spirit within them hasn't
left. They're just sort of ignoring Him at this point. They've
sort of set God aside. They've been to Disneyland for a short
time and they'll come back when the pressures get greatest,
possibly. Prayerfully they will.

But many question whether those restorative forces will operate
today. Pastors have no trouble attesting to the truth of the first

1. *Religion in America 1979-80* (Princeton Religious Research Center, n.d.),
p. 28.

part of the phenomenon—teen-agers do take leave from active church life, any time from the beginning of high school to the college years. But not too many are sure that the stirring of family responsibility will bring the young adults back. Those starting families may find their needs met by a multitude of options, of which the Church is only one. With the erosion of denominational loyalty, there is not the traditional urging to continue the "family Faith."

But for a large number of formerly unchurched interviewed in this study, the pull of family responsibilities did make them look toward the Church. Some felt the need to have their children baptized and/or brought to Sunday School. Occasionally these children were already past the age at which the parents themselves had been baptized or had begun formal religious training. When pastors insisted that the parents attend church themselves before the children could be brought into a formal church relationship, some interviewees were put off. Others responded positively to the imposition of such conditions. In a few instances, the children themselves started attending a neighborhood church alone or with friends. One parent told of his six-year-old daughter visiting different churches on her own before she chose the one she wanted. Her parents were not attending any at the time. Sometimes it was the grandparents who expressed concern and put the pressure on for Baptism and religious education.

The dominant reason that over 30 respondents gave for returning to church was to keep the family together, to strengthen family life. But what if one marital partner had no religious background or interest or even had an anti-Church attitude? In most cases, the unchurched spouse eventually joined under the urging of husband or wife, or the pleading of children. However, one spouse interrupted periodically during the interview with her newly-churched Baptist husband to say that his renewed religious concern had caused a rift in their relationship. More commonly, marrying a devout church member, or experiencing an Encounter weekend, and coming to a new appreciation of the Church's ministries prompted a stirring of faith in the unchurched person which led to church membership.

An example: a professional football player in California who had an on-and-off affiliation with different Churches became a Lutheran because of his wife's faith. He said, "Sure I get something out of church, out of the words. And I really want, to believe. That's why I go. Also, because my wife just had a couple of serious operations, and she vowed that she was going back to church. Whether that's the right reason or the wrong reason, I don't know. The best reason is because you feel that something's void, something's lacking in your life. So I honestly—it was her commitment."

A woman from Huntington Beach, California says her religious background was "really very slender." The fact that she had been divorced disturbed her Catholic husband, she said. They petitioned ten years ago for some adjustment so that they could be married in the Church, but their request was denied. Only in recent years did she speak to a priest again and find that the situation is different today. She and her husband have now joined the Catholic Church. She said, "Had I not been prompted because of my husband's background, we probably wouldn't be where we are today. The way I was raised, I didn't know the good feeling of going to church on Sunday and trying to be part of a parish and part of any organized religion. My husband had such strong feelings, and they were becoming more bitter toward the Church. By bitter, I don't mean unkind, but he was really feeling let down.... I felt kind of responsible for it, so I guess that's why I made the initial contact."

Stanford, a member of a UCC congregation in Lansing, was unchurched until his marriage. "I married a girl that was a very strong member in this church. She'd been coming for 35 years. And she always holds offices and comes over here several times a week, not just on Sundays. After we got married and moved to this area, I started going to the church with her. Then after I retired from Oldsmobile, within two months they put me on the board of trustees in charge of the buildings and also the minister's home. So it was more or less in my line of work—maintenance I like." Although Stanford enjoyed the new association with church people, he made no mention of religious conviction during our long and pleasant interview.

A very different testimony was offered by John, who described his former spiritual ideas and how they were enhanced after his marriage. He notes at first that his faith had been "quite a bit just my own religion." He continued:

> My church was out in the woods. If I had a problem, and I wanted to talk with God, I'd go out and talk with Him, one-on-one, out in the woods or in a field. Then I met Kara. And we just started going to church. It was an easy thing for me to do because I was in love with her and I was in love with God, quite honestly, and she had her way of demonstrating her love for God and I had mine. And mine wasn't that much different from hers. We were married by a Christian Reformed minister who happened to turn out to be a good friend of both of us.

Anita, describing why she and her husband joined a Church in West Virginia's Boone County after being outside for many years, said simply, "I converted for the reason that I had to do what the head of the household said. And he said this is the one."

Marriage problems became so acute for some people that the Church was seen as a last resort. For example, in an attempt to win his estranged wife back, Dane, a worker in the logging mills in Independence, Oregon, started going to church. He described that experience, "So after she moved out, I tried to find out what was bothering her. I went to talk to her mother. Her mother went to church quite a bit, so I got to going with her. Maybe if I went to church with her mother, I thought, she'd move back in. First time I went out there [to the Baptist Church], it seemed like everything the minister was saying, he was talking right to me. Seemed like nobody else was in there." When I asked Dane what was the main thing that brought him to church, he answered, "My wife. We've been married 26 years. I don't think I can get over a marriage like she can. Now with the Lord's help, we can make this one work. I know on my own I can't make it work."

Another Polk County Baptist, Pat, said that for the ten years after he was married, he never set foot inside a church. He described what happened to change him:

> Our problems got so bad that we were both searching for answers. Jane had said, "Why don't we go to a church?" But then when *I* made the suggestion, well, it was pretty good. We just went over for that one day. We were just looking for something, anything. Jane mentioned that she felt better.... It's something that binds you together. There were times when I thought that we were very happily married. But there's been something since then. The love of the Lord—that's just united us in a way that never was before. Without even realizing we were lacking something. It's still hard for me to explain.

Marriage Encounter played a major role in bringing lapsed Catholics into a renewed affiliation with their Church. Encounters which were sponsored by other denominations also touched people at a deep level. The different experiences people described agreed on one point—they had given up on the Church before the Encounter weekend, but when they found that the Church spoke deeply to them in this area of life, they thought maybe the Church had something to say about the rest of their lives.

After Marriage Encounter in California, Fred and Sheryl rejoined the Catholic Church they had been brought up in but had left. Sheryl talked about her husband:

> He went along pretty much because of me and because he knew I want my family to belong, and the kids to know they belong, and to grow up within the framework of it. But within that, he has a love of his own totally unlike mine, so it's very hard for me to understand. But for him it's just as valuable, just as viable. It's—he has a very personal relationship with God. ... We've begun teaching confirmation classes, and sometimes when he talks to these boys it's really neat. He really says a lot.

A couple in Lansing had a varied religious background, each having been affiliated with at least three denominations. Both drifted away about nine years ago. When asked how they wound up in a Lutheran congregation when neither had previously been a member of any Lutheran church, Maria answered:

> Well, I guess there's just one reason, and that's Marriage Encounter. John and I have some good friends that encouraged us to go to Lutheran Marriage Encounter, and as a result of that, we rediscovered not only a basis of love within ourselves, but also a basis of love within the Church. I guess the things that I was not hearing before were there, but I was not tuned in to it. The idea of loving relationships, God's love, was not really close to me. . . . Our whole perspective had changed so that everything had more meaning. We are amazed at the kind of sermons that people could give once we were kind of in tune with that. Whether it was listening to music at a concert or exploring nature more fully. All of it had more meaning. And so sermons and our contacts with other people had more meaning.

Another Michigan couple said that after their Marriage Encounter weekend, they and their children "made a deal, the four of us, that we'd go to churches and we'd try them, and we would make no judgments at all until after church. We would leave, and we would have brunch, and while we were having brunch we'd discuss it." They went to two different congregations, liking the first church, but finding the second "big and cold and nobody spoke to us, and we judged that wasn't the right church." Jill continued, "Then we went to St. Paul's. We didn't even get as far as the door to leave when we were all saying, 'Hey, we want to come back.' And we've just never gone anywhere else."

Children can play a large part in evangelizing parents by stimulating parental concern for their religious education. In some cases the children came home from church or Sunday School and became witnesses—or pests—to their parents. Some adults promised while still in the Sunday sack to go with their children—the next time. More than one person quoted the Isaiah passage "and a little child shall lead them" to describe how their unchurched pattern changed.

Marie, a young woman living near Winfield, Alabama, said that for many years, "I had a close relationship with God. But I did not feel that I wanted the institution, the rules and regulations of a church. So I didn't go." After severe illness brought one of the children close to death, Marie said, "He made it, he came out fine. . . . And I started thinking about my children—especially Matthew—how am I going to teach them anything, what to do according to religion, according to Jesus. I've got to know something, and I didn't know anything. All I knew was my relationship with God, not much of Jesus. So I figured, 'I'll join the Catholic Church, just so I can teach them.' "

Jonathan, a member of the Free Will Baptist Church in Guin, Alabama, had no trouble answering my question on the main thing that led him into a Church. "Them two little girls running around in the yard. That is one of the most important things in our lives, me and my wife both—our two daughters. We want to do what's right for them, to where they will grow up living the right kind of life, and hopefully marry the right kind of man, to where they won't have the trouble and things that other people do have, as far as heartbreaks and divorces."

A woman in Laguna Hills, California who had been brought up Catholic but attended church by herself until her teen years, felt, "If my parents had been members of the Church, it would have made all the difference in the world. But when you're just going on your own, when you get to be a teen-ager there's lots of other things to do." Her husband, a Lutheran, "had church pushed at him too much," she says. "He was just the opposite from me." Grandmother reminded the couple, after children came along, that it was time for Baptism, she remembers. Soon Grandma announced that it was time for the oldest daughter to begin confirmation lessons.

And I thought, "Well, gee, we'd better take care of that." And I didn't think it was right to say, "All right, you have to go over here to this church and take confirmation classes, but we're not going to have anything to do with it." We didn't know where to go. Then one day Dee mentioned that one of the girls in school was a Lutheran, and she went to the Church of the Cross. And I don't think we really had any intention of getting that involved in the Church at that time, but this church is just unbelievable.

She closed our interview by saying, "I feel that I've gotten so much out of our congregation and our Church, I want to share it with everybody else. So I really enjoy the evangelism work."

Bill, a 40-year-old executive at the opposite end of Orange County, said:

> I think one of the biggest and most important things is my children. I definitely want them brought up as Christians, and the Church is obviously the center or the hub for spreading this word, this information, more so than just sitting at home and reading the Bible and trying to interpret it on your own. At church you've got the instructor, the pastor, who can lend meaning to those things that you don't understand. You have the center there to come together with other Christians with similar ideas and obviously the same beliefs. You can talk to people freely about your beliefs and programs and shall we do this and that.

One couple in Searsport, Maine had been interviewed by Russell Hale two years before when they were unchurched. Since that time they joined the Methodist Church in town. During the time they were unchurched, they said they "kinda just found that Sunday was just another day of the week." But when their oldest started to go to Sunday School with another boy, "It just didn't work out. He didn't want to go by himself. We figured at least he needed a Christian education, which he wasn't getting very much at home. So we started going ourselves. We found the Church to be very much of a big family."

A young Oregon couple's church membership began with an invitation thrown at them during the Fourth of July parade. The invitation, wrapped in a Tootsie Roll, invited them to Faith Lutheran Church in Monmouth. After their two small children were enrolled in Sunday School, Dolly and then Rob began attending church. According to Dolly, "We were really at a time when our kids were at an impressionable age, when we wanted to raise 'neat kids.' We're both from divorced families. So we really had to work harder. And then you reach out there and you see something that you want. We found that in the families of the congreation at Faith." They found an additional close fellowship with parents at a Lutheran parochial school 25 miles away. Althought it meant long-distance driving and dividing themselves between two congregations, they valued the closeness of working together with the other parents and strengthening their family and faith life.

Ben, a young unemployed man in Independence, Oregon, had convinced himself in his late teens "that I didn't need to join anything because I still believed." But after marriage and parenthood, "primarily because of the children," he says, "I started wondering where my values had come from—ethics and morals. And I realized a lot of it came from my religious background. I thought that that was important." For a while Ben and his wife still postponed regular attendance at a church. But the change came about,

> partly because of Christa's being five and starting school. And realizing that it was difficult for me to explain to her about Jesus and to pray, without the church background and participation myself. How can I show her and tell the children that it's important, if I don't participate myself? Part of it too was that I always believed in Jesus, and the last few years I would notice things in a different light. I just started noticing that if I was in a close call in a car, or really hard up for money—just about the time I would start to panic, something would come up and straighten out. I began to see those things as more than accidental.

A unique story was told me by a young New York executive, Jack, who had drifted through different main line Protestant Churches in his youth. He dated a "very religious, very devout Catholic. She told me that it seemed like I wasn't at peace with myself. I was always impressed with her own sense of peacefulness." Later, still single, Jack offered his services to Big Brothers as a volunteer and was assigned to a Spanish Pentecostal family. Ten years before the mother had been "born again." Jack said:

> Since I was working with Marcos, seeing Marcos every week, his mother felt it was important that I appreciate what it

means to be a Christian, if not become a Christian myself. . . .
I acquiesced and agreed to do some Bible study with her, just
on a weekly basis. This was about a year and a half. . . . So
we met, and she assigned me a page to read every week and
we came back and discussed it, and lo and behold, I found
myself becoming very interested and intrigued and thinking
a lot about it. She brought me to the point of accepting the
Lord.

Eventually Jack joined a Methodist church in Manhattan. "What
really turned me to the Church," Jack says, "was to really study,
to read the Bible and think about what Christ meant. It was that
focus upon Jesus that was so important to me."

Terry and Frances are new members of the Methodist Church
in Garden Grove, California. Both come from mixed marriages,
Catholic and Protestant. They dropped out of the Church after
they were married, except for an occasional Christmas service:

When our babies came, we went to have them baptized. When
we had moved into this house, the first Christmas we looked
up the closest Methodist church and went to church at Christmas time, and that was about it. And then we went to have
our first child baptized, and then the second one. And our
minister says, "Hey, how come this little one isn't in Sunday
School?" We just looked at each other and thought, "Yeah,
how comes she isn't?" So we started to take her to church—it
was the only reason we started going to church. And then we
became very involved, and we really love it now.

Frances added:

When [the minister] sat down and talked to us, we started
thinking, "Our parents cared enough to raise us in the
Church, and here I was going to raise my kids in the Church."
And then it dawned on me that here she is three years old
and never been to Sunday School. And so we came home and
we had quite a fight. My husband wasn't going to go to
church, and I said, "I'll be darned if I'm going to be one of
those parents that drop their kid off every Sunday." So he
said, "OK, I'll go." That's the only reason we're going. But
it was the kids that did it.

The minister's counseling with this couple before Baptism gave them an opportunity to reflect about where they themselves were with the Church as well as to prepare for the child's Baptism. They remember him saying, "As far as you're concerned, I can talk until I'm blue in the face and I'm not going to make any difference to you guys, but I do want the children in Sunday School. If you want to drop them off, that's fine with me. Your time's already come and gone, but let them have their turn." It might have begun as a totally child-centered concern, but now Frances told me, "If the kids are sick, we'll get a sitter and leave them at home so we can go to church."

While some parents suddenly became aware of responsibility toward their children, others had children who sought out a church home themselves and then began actively to recruit their reluctant parents. Such is the case with the couple living in Searsport, Maine who decided, "The kids were getting old enough for Sunday School." The mother, June, recalls, "The oldest one was three at the time, so we went to this church down here. The kids said, 'We really like this music.' "

Meanwhile, Bertram, the father, had stayed at home. His comment was, "You can go if you want, but I'm not going." That changed, June recalled, when their little three-year-old boy came home from Sunday School and said, "Daddy, that Sunday School down there is for daddies too." "That really started working on him," June added. Bertram explained, "Oh, I just went to please the kids the first time. Like she said, when I was there for one service, it was just like something drew you back to the next one. What it was, was the presence of God, that's all. I knew it. Just the minute I went in, there was no doubt about it in my mind at all."

Tom, a policeman from New York City, told me:

My daughter at one point in her life—six years old—she wanted to go to Sunday School. Then they asked if we might like to come and help paint the Sunday School room because our child was attending. And they said that there would be an informal Eucharist and a dinner afterwards. Wear old clothes, and we'd get to painting afterwards. And we came, had a very informal Eucharist in the cloister chapel, dinner together, painted together. It was a very enjoyable evening. We never stopped coming.

In that Episcopal Church, Tom had "a personal experience, a personal awakening, that happened to me and that was the turning point which in my own life pointed and called me to a ministry." His plans are to pursue that ministry in the police force. He attends theology classes, fitting them between his shifts at the police station.

A new member of the First Church [UCC] in Belfast, Maine says, "My daughter decided she would like to go to Sunday School. I felt that if she was going to Sunday School, I was the one who was going to church. I would not take her and drop her and pick her up afterwards. I do not believe in that. That's basically one reason. And another is that times have changed, and I think that maybe religion is the only thing that is actually basically going to stay when you need it and where you need it."

Harold, a solidly built workingman in his forties, was another new member of the Searsport evangelical group. He said quite frankly:

The only reason I started to go, really, was my children. My wife started going about two years before I did. I used to go once in a while. Then my daughter, the one you just met here, came in one morning as I was lying in bed and asked me if I was going to church today. I said that I wasn't. She asked me "Why not?" I said—kind of grouchy—that I didn't want to. She looked at me and she said "What's the matter, dad? Don't you know the Lord?" That kind of got to me. I said, "Yes, of course I do." She said, "Well, how come you're not going to church?" I didn't have any answer for her then. They went to church, I didn't go. But either the next Sunday or the Sunday after that, I started going. Then I accepted the Lord as my Savior. I've been going ever since.

His wife, Esther, added:

It seemed like after we were married we were happy together, and I loved him and we had a nice family. I loved my family and it seemed like I had everything. But inside, I had nothing. I just felt empty. Our oldest daughter, she used to go to the Congregational Church to Sunday School. We always made sure the kids went to Sunday School, even though we didn't go. And I never wanted to go to church. I thought, "That's not for me. I don't ever want to go." Even though I was unhappy and was searching in all different directions to find happiness, I just couldn't find it. Well, she started going over here to Sunday School, Searsport Full Gospel. One Sunday she asked me to go. She used to ask me a lot—she was only about seven or eight. Finally I said, "I'll go with you just once. But I'll never go back again, so don't ask me." So I went that one Sunday, and I'd never been in a Church in my life that preached the Gospel. Every Church—if they did, I never heard it, really. This Church was different and I felt a love in that Church that I never felt before in my life. The pastor asked people if they wanted to accept Christ as their Savior. I had heard this on TV, but it had never sunk in, I guess. I put my hand up, but I didn't dare to go forward. Something stopped me, but I've been going to church ever since. I think it was the Sunday after that that I went forward and accepted Christ. And it just changed my life so much. I've been so happy. There is nothing like it. I wouldn't go back to the life I'd lived before for anything.

Another Maine woman, living far from town in a simple house in rolling hills near Winterport, said that Sunday morning often meant nursing a hangover from Saturday night. When she rebuffed her son's invitation to go to church with him, she remembers he said to her, "Mom, if you don't love God, I can't make you." She continued, "And he left the room. From then on I've been going to church. Since that minute I get right up, get ready. I never had any intention of going in the first place, so you know that God really brought me down to that church. God used my son to speak to me to get me down there. I had the Baptism of the Holy Spirit and it's just been the most beautiful thing that's ever happened to me.

Several interviewees referred to relationships with their aged parents as the cause for their renewed interest in the Church. A woman in Dallas, Oregon said, "Jim's mother, who's very religious and was a fine woman, got cancer and died within three weeks. We decided it probably would have been her wish that we all attend church and have the children baptized. So we just went up here in the summertime—Pastor F was on vacation—and just started going and started making friends. He gave us instruction and we joined a year later." She recalled that it was her husband's initiative that led them to church for the first time. "It was just something that he wanted to—he kept talking about wanting to get back into the Church and everything, and we'd say, 'Well, yes, maybe next Sunday,' you know. We'd rather sleep in and read the paper. So finally he said, 'OK. This is the Sunday, and we're going to get up, and we're going to get dressed, and we're going.' And so that's just exactly what we did, and we haven't regretted it."

A minister of the Christian Methodist Episcopal Church in Sarasota reflected a general impression when he said, "We strive for a large Sunday School attendance, because 90 percent of the time if you get the black males in their youth . . . . Now they may detour when they get into teen-ages and young adults, but once they get married, they'll always—I'll say nine out of ten times—they'll always be coming back to the Church. But you have to get them in their youth. They'll always return. But if you don't get them in that time, then it's very, very hard to get them." He convinced his congregation that in spite of all the problems inherent in a bus ministry, a bus was necessary to pick up children who would have had no other way of attending. To say that the children are the Church of tomorrow may be cliche. But that doesn't mean it isn't true.

It would be worthwhile to ascertain the reasons why formerly churched parents, now outside the fold, do not take responsibility toward the religious upbringing of their children. Also, what would trigger a renewed church commitment on the part of young people who, though married, prefer to remain childless? How do singles deal with the "rooting" process as they become part of a community? What factors attract them to or repel them from the

Church? A study of singles entitled *Saturday Night, Sunday Morning* shows how the family-centered congregation looks from the outside, from the viewpoint of a single person.[2] Do young people who live together outside of marriage feel that they can have any welcome in a Church? In what ways can the Church reach out to people who do not follow the usual pattern of marriage and parenthood? What can be done to shorten their period of "vacation" from the Church? These are questions for another study.

THE SEARCH FOR COMMUNITY

People who step into a new Church setting deserve a lot of credit. It takes a strong dose of courage to enter a group as an outsider. There is the unfamiliarity of a group of people, a building with unknown doors and well-hidden rest rooms, a preacher who doesn't know the stranger, perhaps a liturgy with all sorts of mysterious risings and sittings. One Catholic priest put it this way, " 'Welcome' is one of the big things. There's nothing worse than being in an intimate group—on the outside. And everybody is hugging, and you don't know anybody. It's a terrible feeling. The way we become elitist is when we become comfortable and not welcoming."

Community—from the Greek *koinonia*—can be a goal easier to define than to attain. One interviewee from Oregon said that he attended a local Presbyterian church four Sundays in a row without once being greeted by anyone in that congregation. His family then went to another Presbyterian church several miles from home. They found there a warmth and welcome that encouraged them to come back and join. Probably some less motivated people would have given up after the first or second try.

What made the difference between the two church experiences? Does a congregation have its own personality? Could one take its temperature reading: cool, warm, hot? Or is welcome merely an accident depending on whom one sits next to? You could feel a warm welcome because someone greets you, explains where the

2. Nick Christoff, *Saturday Night, Sunday Morning* (San Francisco; Harper & Row, 1978).

order of service is, and chats after service time. Or it could be missing because someone shy or disinterested just turns away. An isolated experience might wrongly or rightly be generalized to the whole congregation.

A pastor can easily build a word-picture of a loving fellowship and give strong biblical reasons for working toward such a goal. But it is more difficult for the pastor to experience himself what it really means to be a stranger in his own church. His status alone assures him of some response—even on his first Sunday.

Of the many factors that lead unchurched people to church membership, fellowship is one that seems most ripe for implementing. We can't manufacture crises in peoples' lives, nor can we easily manipulate family pressures to nudge someone closer to the church doors. But there may be ways to raise the consciousness of church members to empathize with the stranger and observe some rules of church sociability.

A friendly atmosphere—however that can be measured—made some interviewees feel at home when they visited a church. It bespoke a relationship that was warmer and deeper than they had experienced in non-church groups. Strangers, new in the congregation, somehow felt welcome. It was easy to return. In East Lansing, Kathy, a recent convert to the Presbyterian Church, was asked why she chose her new church home. She answered, "I thought the people were real nice, and they are fairly intellectual people who are aware of different things. And they seem to be really willing to learn, and they take on challenges. And I just really liked them a lot. They were very, very friendly and warm to new members. And it is a pretty large church."

A member of the Garden Grove Community Church in California praised its friendliness. Asked, "Is it strange belonging to a great big church like Garden Grove?" Walter replied, "It's not . . . there's a lot of bodies, but it's a very small church. Everybody is extremely friendly. The reason, I think, is that it's so large that nobody knows who the membership is. Therefore, everybody's friendly with everybody, because they don't know if they're visitors, members, or what. Plus they have small groups all week long. I enjoy going to the breakfast. We have a Wednesday morning prayer breakfast. I go to that every week. I'm there at 6:30."

Several interviewees described their congregation in terms of an extended family. Some said that they felt closer to church members than they did to their relatives. That probably says something both about the congregations and about their relatives.

Two members of the Church of God of Prophecy were in the Christian Coffee House set up in the basement of a store in Winfield, Alabama when I talked with them on a weekend evening. They had been outside the Church for several years. Both of them spoke of what fellowship meant to them. Said Hal, "Well, church to me is kind of a social organism. When I say that, I don't mean that a church is like a country club or anything like that. But man is by nature a social animal. No man is an island. He draws strength from others that are like him." Diane agrees, "Well, love too. You need family love. After you're born again, all those other people that are born again—they're your family, really. I love my mother and daddy and everything, but they don't go to church. They're one of those unchurched groups. The Church just means a lot. I know that every church you go to, it couldn't be like this, but—those people at ours, anyway, they're just full of love and everything. It's like we're just one big happy family. . . . It's really just like the whole Body of Christ."

A member of the Methodist Church in Garden Grove, Frank said he would tell an unchurched person that his congregation is "a very loving place. It's a warmth. It's a place . . . it's our family. And if you like us, then you're going to like the rest of us. If you sit in my living room and you like talking to me, then you're going to like the people over here, because they're exactly like me. So come and join our family." A business woman in Maine said, "Christ means everything to me, but my church is very important, because it's where I found Christ. If we're ever going to move away—I've thought of this before—I would miss my church more than my family, more than my physical family."

Some respondents indicated that they found companionship in the Church. They spoke of loneliness and of how the Church has filled a gap for them. An attractive middle-aged mother in Laguna Hills, California talked about the fellowship she experienced after she joined a local congregation:

> I really get a lot out of it. Well, companionship for one thing. . . . belonging. I think that's very important, especially nowadays when you can't even visit your friends without a written invitation, because everybody's so wrapped up in their own tiny world, and they don't want you butting in. So it's very hard to really belong anywhere except to your own Family. And I think in a church you have a feeling of belonging and being with other people that feel the same way you do about things. And it's a very nice feeling.

Nicolle gives a lot of credit to the pastor:

> When I started going to his church over here, I got warmth and companionship and the caring which is something that really fascinated me about the pastor. I wasn't just another number, or another name on the rolls or whatever. He really cared about us as individuals, as a family, and that really came across. And that made a big impression on me which started me going to church. And it's just something that evolved by itself. It wasn't an overnight, all of a sudden, "Hallelujah" type of thing. It evolved very gradually. Maybe it was just the repetition of hearing it over and over, week after week, but it finally started to sink in. I got to the point where I was beginning to believe certain things. And it's still going on. As far as I'm concerned, it's an on-going process.

A young member of Calvary Chapel in Costa Mesa, California talked with me after a packed 7:30 a.m. service. Annette said this of the fellowship:

> This is where I met people who would teach me what it meant to walk with Him, and who would be patient with me when I made mistakes. This became my family. That's really important, that a Church is a spiritual family. Especially in today's society when families are falling apart. To come to a place that is like a family is really necessary. So by that time, I guess. I learned the voice of God to the point where

He could say, "This is where I want you to stay and grow up."
So I said, "OK."

Laile, a recent convert to the Episcopal Church in Sarasota, said about her affiliation, "I feel it's filling a void in my life. Not just spiritually, but providing me, frankly, with other outlets that I had not even looked for, such as the happiness of singing with the choir, meeting new friends, and so on."

Ron and Lorrie, who were won to the Church by the evangelism efforts of a Lutheran congregation in Holt, Michigan, said that the factors that led them to the Church included a need for fellowship. Lorrie explained, "A lot of it was wanting to have lasting friendships, because you think of all your high school friends that have since moved away. And the friendships that I have had before were nothing, even back in the parochial school. I don't see any of the kids anymore, and I really needed and wanted friendship other than my family. And I think that's what I was seeking, and so I looked for it in a church."

The social life for some is an opportunity to share—to give and to receive. For example, a young couple in Costa Mesa, California admitted that they had had little religious training as children. Bill said that he had gone to Sunday School "off and on" till he got tired of going. "I lost interest in it entirely," he remembers. Through a bus ministry all their five children were enrolled in a neighborhood Sunday School. With encouragement from the bus driver, Bill began attending the Assembly of God Church. For him this conversion was a dramatic story which had to be shared within the close fellowship of his congregation:

Wednesday meeting I got up and told the congregation—really they're our family—that I cannot make one single day without God. I cannot live one day without God. I love Jesus. I love God. For the first time in my life. And I feel that part of this is because of the people in the Church, that they're part of the family of God. They just put their arms out to you, they reach out to you. They welcome you. They'll talk to you when church is over, they talk to you during the church. They call you by name, which is important to everybody, and they don't forget your name. And they're always happy to see you.

They'll look you right in the eye, and you can tell they're
genuinely happy to see you. They enjoy you, and this is what
made me want to work for them. I feel like I'm serving God,
but I'm also serving my family. I'm working for them and
I enjoy this. I want to do this. And really can't do enough.

Helen remembers why she joined a Baptist church in Oregon. "I
really enjoy the people and wanted to be in fellowship with
them." Her husband added, "The first thing that came to my
mind was the fellowship. This is still something that is hard for
me to express. You may be completely off-base, completely
wrong. You may get into a nice discussion with someone, but when
you leave there you become a lot closer to that person. They won't
put you down . . . for your feelings."

Fellowship is experienced by some as help in their time of
need. One interviewee who spoke of fellowship described "the
helpfulness of the people. When you need someone, you have to
turn to one of our brothers." A residential home builder in California found in his evangelical congregation a community based
on more than just friendly worship services. He said:

There was a need in our life, and we both knew it, and God
pointed the finger in the right direction. And now we don't
say, "What are we going to do? And where are we going?
What's the future?" Now there is a future—something to look
forward to, because all people in church can help you in one
way or another, and they have. Like one is in real estate, and
maybe one is a carpenter, and one is an electrician and one
is a plumber. If you want to build a house or buy a house
or whatever, somebody will advise you, help you, do something. And there's always some kind of help in the church,
no matter what you need. Whether it's spiritual or financial
or whatever it is. And they'll do it, they'll help you, because
they believe in us. They believe in us all the way; they love
and they're happy that we're with them, and we're happy to
be with them.

It surprised me to find members of the Garden Grove Community Church, with its membership of about 10,000, talking
about what a close, warm fellowship they found. A new member
who travels quite a distance to get there said:

Yes, it's farther away than many of the churches locally, but there is a dynamic force in this church. There is a joyous sense of giving and caring, where religion is not hellfire and damnation. It is rather a marvelous, uplifting, wonderful, enlightening, mind-expanding experience. There is a warmth and caring friendliness in the members of the church I have never encountered anywhere before...That's what the Church, to me, is all about. It's friends when you need them, people to share your faith. People to be with you in a joyous celebration of faith in God, instead of "Oh boy, I've sinned."

Her son, 18, who had been hospitalized for critical surgery, added, "There are so many beautiful people who said, 'Man, we were praying for you.' It just gives you such a beautiful feeling when you hear that, especially in today's society. Because so many people have lost the ability to care and understand."

Some interviewees talked about the honesty and integrity of church people who do what they say they believe. This made the fellowship solid for them. Wayne, a young member of the Church of God of Prophecy near Winfield, Alabama, described the difference in his earlier life between what the Church taught and how he lived. He said that he tried to justify himself and his own lack of interest in the Church by blaming people whom he judged to be hypocrites. After he was humbled by his own sense of need, he looked at the church fellowship in a new way. He explained:

A lot of different things happened mostly when I found the church was people...when I knew the people were sincere. I'd never been to a church where people were sincere—lived what the Church taught. And I came to know a few other young people really well and grew real close to them and knew that they lived their everyday lives the way I thought a Christian should. I found that at the Church of God that I go to. We have an everyday experience with the Lord that a lot of young people don't know that they can have.

A young couple in Searsport, Maine described the difference between their former church and the Full Gospel Congregation. Bertram explained:

With the other church, we'd go out dancing and drinking and the same people would be there who'd been in church, and you wouldn't feel any conviction about anything like that. I mean, everybody but the pastor was up there. But then Sunday morning, they'd be so stuck up, they wouldn't speak to you. The night before they were all friendly, friendly. There's one thing in our present church that I notice now . . . the extreme friendliness. You know, people come up and shake your hand, and at first I'd almost think "What are you doing? How come you're doing that?" It was really strange to me.

Bertram's wife, June, remembers her apprehension over attending this Pentecostal congregation. "One of the first times I went in, I sat 'way in the back because I had told my friend, 'If anything weird goes on, I'm leaving. I'm sitting right near the door so I can run.' And the pastor came down off the platform and shook my hand before I even had a chance to move. And I thought, 'Boy, that's strange.' He was really good. He was really personally friendly."

Some people talked about the Church's loving fellowship as expressed by physical affection. Hank, a member of the Church of the Nazarene, described different Churches he'd attended. Some were filled with a loving warmth, others lacked it. He said:

Once you're in the Church, been in the loving fellowship of the Church, you find that your family doesn't mean as much to you; your relationship to a family doesn't mean as much as the church family does. There's just a kind of a feeling there—just a love, and the love bonds. Whether it's with a handshake or a hug, or even in some cases kisses and stuff. The love is very open and undemanding, and you can say something and not worry about stepping on someone's toes or saying something you shouldn't or being afraid that someone else is going to hear about it. Just to be very open and honest. . . . That we enjoy very much.

Tom and Janice, members of the Methodist Church in Searsport, Maine, reported how much their church fellowship means to them:

It's nice to be in a group of people who believe the same

belief and are trying to bring their children up and lead their lives in the same way. You just get a close, warm feeling; you feel like saying more things, talking to them more than you do to strangers, really. After your whole routine is done, after five or six days, and you're really down in the dumps, you can go in. This is a chance where you get to see everybody. Everybody is feeling the same way, and it just seems to boost your whole morale so you know you can go through another week.

A new member of the Metropolitan Community Church in Sarasota, a divorced father with two children, spoke of holding on tenaciously to his church:

Ever since I walked through that front door, off of Washington Boulevard: I have known nothing but total joy, love, feelings I've never experienced before, and in different connotations also. Love to me was something that you read about— I had never experienced love—I'm not counting the love that I have for my kids, I'm using a different context. I'm more at peace with myself, with others. There's just no way I can tell you exactly what I feel here. It's a strange feeling, it's a new feeling, but I'm not going to give it up, there's no way I'm going to give it up.

For some respondents, new membership in a congregation meant a new circle of friends. This happened intentionally as church people took up more of their time. For others there was a sadder result; they sensed a distance from their unchurched friends who didn't understand the new fellowship. A few people said that they missed former friends who had turned their backs; others said they tried to reach out and share, only to have these friends back off. A few tried successfully to maintain old friendships in spite of a lack of communication with respect to their new-found religious insights and enthusiasm.

In Orange County's Calvary Chapel, I joined 200 men one Thursday morning at 7:00 for a prayer breakfast. Some well-dressed young men sitting next to me engaged in polite conversation, asking me who I was and what I was doing. When I described the project I was working on, one man asked, "Why do you think most people are unchurched?" I used Russell Hale's book as authority and responded, "The largest group of the un-churched claim that there are too many hypocrites in the Church." The young man slapped his thigh and said, "You know, they're right. We're all hypocrites in the Church. Not one of us is living the kind of life God wants him to live. But we're in the Church to get the forgiveness and grace to do better." That was a commonly-shared feeling at the prayer breakfast. It was an hour of fellow-ship, prayer and sharing. It was a living of the Church as loving fellowship—and receiving strength at the beginning of the day to do better.

South of Sarasota city, a Presbyterian pastor, John Bressler, talked of his concept of ministry and how he tried to convey it to the congregation. "I came in trying to say to the folks, my con-cept of the Church is human beings. This is a place where we meet, but this is not the limit. Our operational area is out there in the community. But we learn to do this by becoming a family. We learn all over again what it's like to love one another in a family way and to care for one another and really be intimate." Nurturing this "affectional Church" as he calls it, the pastor, on the Sunday when I joined the worshipers, charged the congregation with their responsibilities as he was receiving new members. In addition to recommending spiritual care in general terms, he asked the estab-lished members aloud if they would, as the Lord suggested, visit these people if they got into trouble and landed in prison. It was a thought I had not considered before. It gave some substance to the idea of fellowship.

Another Presbyterian pastor, in Orange County, said that at the beginning of the service, "One of the first things I ask them to do is send loving thoughts to someone in this congregation. And this is a meditative thing to do." He added:

We're trying to develop our inner strengths, inner life of the fellowship, nurturing one another, then from that point on let it extend into the community. This church would represent a kind of counterpart to the old extended family. I think the Church has to intentionally look at itself more peculiarly in that light, and not be just a place where people come to-gether and get band-aids. Individuals must feel that they're nourished for another week, and during the week we're not only thinking about what the pastor said, but we're thinking about someone else in that congregation's concern. To be conscious of your brother and his needs and loving him unconditionally is what grace is all about. It's a real source of power.

PERSONAL CRISIS

Personal crises challenged the closed world-view of a large number of respondents, causing them to question their lifestyles. In some cases the crisis led to a dramatic conversion. The crisis might be illness, the death of a loved one, a drug overdose, a brush with the law, the loss of a job, a divorce or some vague constellation of circumstances described by one person in these terms: "My universe fell apart." Such events prompted a reordering of priorities and values, and a reaching out for help to meet needs not experienced before.[3]

Several of the younger interviewees had succumbed to increased drug dependency. One recalled being carried into the hospital emergency room after a drug overdose. Another smoked marijuana so regularly that she saw it as a constant source of security for her future years, imagining herself sitting in a rocker on the porch at 90—still smoking pot. One day she began to feel alarm over her dependency on her "pacifier."

Some people that were interviewed described their situation as "losing control." Everything had been under control for them; suddenly their hand was shaken, and they lost the ability to order their lives. They became vulnerable. They sought help from outside themselves. A young man in Hackleburg, Alabama described his experience:

Really I was enjoying things until they began to corrupt my life. I became a drug-addict, or nearly a drug-addict, after

3. Dr. Win Arn, of the Institute for American Church Growth, has produced a "Receptivity-Rating Scale" showing the relative importance of crises for a person's responsiveness to change. He suggests that a period of transition is a span of time in which an individual's or family's normal everyday behavior patterns are disrupted by some irregular event that requires an unfamiliar response. Dr. Arn's chart will be found in *Church Growth: America* (Summer, 1978), p. 3.

many years of being away from Sunday School. At the age of 17, I was experiencing many things such as jail, drugs and so forth, and it really brought a downfall in my life. Through that God allowed me to see that I really needed Him, and that I really needed an experience with Jesus, that I really needed to face the reality that I could be nothing without Him.

Calvary Chapel in Costa Mesa, California, under the leadership of Pastor Chuck Smith, has shown a deep concern for young people whose lives were getting out of control because of drugs. Two young men told me what the Church did to help them turn a corner. Jim recalls that he wanted to get close to God. "I would think to myself that I had to change," he said, "but the change never came. I was more involved in the life I was living at the time." When asked what made the change come about, Jim answered:

I think it was through drugs. Experimenting with different drugs and getting high. . . . A lot of bummers I went through and seeing what was going on around me—the pollution and how people were. I just started seeing a lot of things. I know it wasn't me. I think that God sort of opened my eyes to all these things. . . . One night I was having some kind of a weird experience with these drugs. I couldn't breathe, because I was smoking some hash, and I heard a voice saying that I was going to die. I got a little scared, and I started praying. The way I was living, the drugs and all that, I knew it wasn't right. I knew because of my upbringing in the Catholic Church that if I was to die in that condition, I would go to hell. It really scared me. I met some Christians in the handball court. They told me about giving my life to the Lord. I knew they were right, but I was just afraid to give up the things that I had.

Some people told him about Calvary Chapel, he remembers, "So I came here. And I just felt the love flow. I never saw anyting like that before in my whole life. . . . I saw the freedom here—it was beautiful."

Another member, Troy, recalled his overdose in junior high, "I knew that God had something to do with me staying alive from my overdose. So in the hospital I just kind of said a little prayer to God. And I asked God 'If You really do have a reason for me being alive, which I didn't know, then show me.' And I'd just kind of keep an eye on Him." At a drug party in the park all of his friends were arrested, Troy explains. His mother picked him up and brought him home. Then, "I began to see my life going down the tubes and away from me, rather than anything constructive at all. I prayed and asked God to forgive me and give me a new life right there. I was sick of the life that I was living, and I asked Him to come into my life and change me. And by the time I sat up in bed—He'd come in; but I didn't know what it was at all."

His brother returned from a summer camping program of Calvary Chapel. He too had been encountered by God. "He came back from that summer camp a totally different man, completely changed. That night I was having a drug party for a friend of mine. The guy I was having the party for accepted the Lord. My brother told him about Jesus, and he accepted the Lord right there, in the middle of the party." Troy was asked to go to Calvary Chapel the next weekend. "When we got there, there were people waiting outside the door to get in. And I thought to myself, 'This is weird. Look, everybody is standing there looking like they're excited to get in.' I had never seen anything like that before in my life. Just looking at the people—they looked like regular people, but there was something different about them. I knew at that moment that something spoke at my heart. It said, 'Troy, your search is over.' "

Troy said that this began a new life for him. I asked him, "How'd you make out with the drugs?" This was his answer:

I quit. You see, this is something that a lot of drug people don't know. I mean rehabilitation centers. And that is, no one can give up something that is—if someone is sitting there thinking that drugs are out of sight, and they just give it up, they're always going to go back to it, because it is good, they like it. That's what they like to do. If they replaced the drugs with, say, a fervency for bowling—all of a sudden bowling is going to take the place of the drugs. With me, I had met something far superior, far better, a far better high. And I knew

what I had was real, it wasn't an illusion, I wasn't deceived.
I wasn't wandering around lost. And so drugs just didn't seem
anything to hold on to. They just weren't worth it anymore.

A young couple in Belfast, Maine recalled their involvement with
drugs in the years just before and after they were married. Art
testified:

> I got into drugs. I was really spastic. I was heavy into smok-
> ing dope. Then we got married. We'd lived together for four
> years. We just kept getting worse and worse, more miserable
> towards each other. We knew there had to be a change. So we
> changed our lives. Well, we didn't . . . the Lord changed our
> lives for us. We realized there was a void in our lives. We'd
> tried what I felt was everything but God. I'm not saying that
> the drugs didn't satisfy me, because they did, temporarily.
> But I feel as if a human being is longing for complete satisfac-
> tion, totally, all of the time. Not just a little bit at a time,
> because that just gives you an itch to want more. You don't
> find full satisfaction until you find the Lord.

When severe sickness strikes us or someone close to us, it may
make us reach out for the first time in a long while for some
power that we can barely imagine. Our boat is going down, the
walls are falling, the ground is giving way—we plead for help.

Marie, a resident of Winfield, Alabama, said the main thing
that led her to seek a relationship with the Church was "my son's
illness." She explained:

> It taught me a lesson, showed me a great reality. It hit me in
> the face. It said, "You have to do something for me, because
> I'm doing something for you. You've always been backwards
> and I'm showing you—and now do something special for me."
> It finally came to me that God loved me so much that He
> used my son to teach me a lesson. He put him on the border
> of death to show me that I've got to do something. I've got to
> change my ways, and I have to do something back. I knew if
> that baby lived, I'd have to do something back.

Patty, a woman in her thirties married to a professional athlete
in Orange County, had always put down Churches as being money-
grubbers. "Their total output to the congregation was trying to

build a new wing for the education department or a new something," she said. But through a personal crisis her attitude changed. "What happened was, I got a tumor on my breast and I had to have it removed, and it was cancer. And I lay there one day and—I don't know if it was like the post-operative blues—all of a sudden I looked at the wall and I thought, 'I really need God and I need to go to church.' So I said that if I got out of this, I was going back to church." Patty was able to share her new Lutheran Church affiliation with her husband and then with others—something that she thought she would never be able to do.

Brad, a 19-year-old in California, had brain hemorrhages that eventually necessitated surgery. While in the hospital preparing for surgery:

> I started to get so scared, I was just really frightened. And all of a sudden a beautiful, warm feeling came over my body, and a voice inside of my head said, "I don't want you to worry, Brad. I'm here and I'm going to see you through." And it was beautiful. I knew it was the Holy Spirit right there in the room with me, just looking over me. All of a sudden it was just this warm, beautiful feeling. It just came over my body and all the strange, scary feeling left, and I began to cry. And I truly believe that to be when He entered my life.

One of the assistant pastors at Garden Grove Community Church telephoned Brad at the hospital. Soon the whole congregation became involved with Brad during his critical hospital stay:

> It just so happened that concurrent with my coming out of the surgery they were having a special prayer session for me at the church. As I came out of it in recovery the use of my left side came back, and the doctors don't know why that happened. It just came back. So there's more proof positive that there's someone besides just man working on me. . . . I don't really think that I could have gone through it if I hadn't joined the Church and become a Christian. I don't think I could have gone through it nearly as well as I did. And so it really meant a lot for me to be able to believe and trust God completely through all of this thing. He brought me through it.

May, a baptized Catholic, had dropped away after high school. She visited the Catholic Student Parish at Michigan State University. "I guess another tragedy sort of brought me to the Church again. My cousin, who was in Vietnam and recently divorced, had committed suicide, and I was really upset. So I came to the church that night. Fr. T was there, and he talked to us . . ." Recalling that it was after her father's death that she fell away from the Church, May continued, "It's sort of odd, because I fell away from a family tragedy and then came back through one too."

Suzannah and I sat in a portico of a Florida Episcopal church. She said that her mother's death seven years before began a process that led her to membership in that congregation. "It took me a long time to get here," she explained. "But perhaps Mom's death and shaking up my world—the carefully constructed universe was falling apart, and it took me a long time to work through all the less effective things, and come to the one that is effective."

Rod and Laurie, a southern California couple, admitted that they, like other people in their neighborhood, had been involved with "anything that keeps them from going to church." I asked what happened to make them change. This was Rod's answer:

With us, we lost a baby. That would probably be the big step. The first thing, actually before the baby was born, we started attending church. I was a boozer, and I got nailed for drunk driving. After 20 solid years of one-eyed driving, they caught me. I was probably never so humiliated in my life. I had the standard thing—all the money I needed—I had everything, you know, but I just didn't have the one little thing. I was lying in this jail cell. In fact, I gave them so much trouble that they threw me in what they called a "hole." Not just a standard cell, the "hole."

Laurie responded to his story, "I had reached the point where I was so totally frustrated with Rod's drinking that I felt I was tired of the good life, OK? Because the good life is great, but it doesn't give you anything to hang on to. So I really had this tremendous feeling, I had tried everything else, and I thought the only thing I can really go back to is God. So I had started going to church and I had been going about four months, and then Rod started going." Rod interjected, "You guys used to leave me in bed. I was too sick." Rod quit drinking, and a few months later the couple had a son. It was the first boy born into Rod's family in almost fifty years. For Laurie, "It was such a—we just couldn't believe that we had finally gotten a son. Rod really thought this was—God had rewarded him."

A rare medical problem killed the baby within just a few days. Laurie continued, "So then Sunday night before services, we went forward, and they [Garden Grove Community Church] have a candlelight garden of prayer where you can go more or less at the evening service. They have rededication. So we totally rededicated our life and became totally new persons. So it's just an entirely new way of life. We still enjoy the good life; we love sailing and things like that, but church always comes first." Their story ended, like Job's of old, with new blessings. They became parents of another son, to join two daughters. Rod testified, "There is just a tremendous peace that God gives you and you just have to realize that this is just part of a plan—part of a special plan that He must have for you."

Some people, particularly the young, talked of undergoing a disintegration of their well-ordered, personal universes. David, a young man who had traveled around as a musician, said that it was in his mind that the Church was only for middle-aged people. "And I thought," he continued, "that I was guaranteed 20 to 30 years, anyway. So I had to get down, desperate, everything fell apart. Everything that I was looking for fell apart. I said, 'O Lord, if that happened according to your will, let me see my need.' Then I started seeking. I found that that's what I needed, that's what I should of had all my life. I wish I'd been in the Church all my life." David returned to Marion County, Alabama, and manages a shop that sells religious music and books. He is a member of the Church of God of Prophecy and helps run its weekend coffee house.

Rob, an active new member of his Lutheran congregation in Holt, Michigan, felt that God had led him through a series of events which formed a plan directing him toward the Church. Following high school graduation, Rob recalled, "I took off thinking, 'Hey you! You're really something great, and you've done this yourself.'" Later, after he had begun tasting failure in different ventures, Rob noted:

> I became aware of those failures, and so I realized what a heap of nothingness I really was, and that I needed someone other than myself. Different people had shared with me before, but I was still up here somewhere and I hadn't reached the low point. Hadn't been dragged to the bottom of the pit, so to speak. And so God wasn't finished with me. He had to take me through these things—the experience of divorce, the experience of failure in school, failure in jobs, and it was then that I was ripe. I didn't have any place else to turn, and I realized I wasn't really that great. And I could turn to the Lord.

Judy, a new member of the Free Will Baptist Church in Guin, Alabama, talked about the depression that led her to the Church. "Our marriage was in trouble, and we had two small children, and things were just not working out. I couldn't work things out for myself, and I was in a deep depression. I was going to a doctor. Then this woman showed interest in me and showed love toward me and got me in church. And I got saved."

Cheryl, who has a responsible position in a California financial institution, recalled that her divorce was an intense crisis for her. "And it's when my spirituality probably reached its peak," she said, "when I gave up, knowing that I had no control and stood out here and screamed, 'Jesus Christ, where in hell are you in my life?' Because of a very physical presence of Christ... I was answered and I thought, 'I had no control. He's here.' I turned the lights off for the first time in six weeks." Cheryl renewed her Lutheran membership in a congregation in Huntington Beach, California.

After his divorce, Henry was invited to Garden Grove Community Church for its singles' program, but he remembers his initial decision to attend a church, "I think certainly it would be the hurt in the divorce, and something that happened 'like that.' It really surprised me; I didn't know about it. It just—Boom!—happened. And I was really shook. And I didn't immediately go to this church, I really immediately started going back to the Baptist Church regularly. But I needed something."

Andrea recalled leaving the Church feeling that "they were full of hypocrisy—the usual cracker-barrel atheist nonsense, you know." She continued:

> But about 1972 we were having marriage problems then, and Leonard remarked that there was this person I had never forgiven, and he was right, of course. But the problem at the moment was I had to forgive him for some things, and I didn't know how to do it. So it all sort of hit at once, and it seemed to me that the Church is the place that understands forgiveness. So I hiked myself over to All Saints [Episcopal Church]. And it was a very stunning experience. So everything was immediately different.... It changed everything, and I think it seemed to me when you hit bottom, that's when you sort of realized—you're not trying to save face anymore, whether you would or would not go to church. But if there seems to be an answer there, to something you're asking, then you go.

She described what happened as almost a conversion experience. "It was funny, I didn't say where I was going, when I shot out that day. I had an impulse to just drive away into the sunset, but I didn't. I drove over there, and I feel incredible."

A FEELING OF EMPTINESS

Sophisticated, well-educated people spoke of a sense of existential anomie, angst, almost despair. Simpler folk talked of "something missing." Those with a poetic streak could say, "I had space." All may have been referring to an aching, long-festering sense of hurt or a sudden discovery of great loneliness. Over a dozen of the interviewees noted a "feeling of emptiness." Some were surprised—everything was in place and going so well, all of the "things" were accounted for—but the gnawing emptiness was still there. One of the church fathers spoke of a "God-shaped blank" which might be filled with a lot of substitutes for God. But it is one in which only God really fits.

Steve, who lives right next to the Free Will Baptist Church in Guin, Alabama, came no closer to it for many years. He explained his feelings, "Well, I knew there was something lacking in my life. I was searching, and I seemed to be searching on the wrong side of the fence. And I knew a longing. The big change was brought about by people in this church who seemed interested in my soul. They came to me and talked to me about it, told me there was a different side from what I was living."

Lorna, another new member of the Guin congregation, said, "I knew there had to be something else in life besides just the day-to-day." Thinking again about the question, "What is the main thing that brought you to the Church at this time?" she answered, "A feeling of no hope—nothing to look forward to. The thought of death scared me. We had a lot of family problems. We got married young, and we had problems like everybody else. And I knew that I wanted something else for us. I know that I wanted our home to stay together. I didn't think I could do it without the Lord's help. And it's really been great the past two years."

Following the inquiry class of St. Martha's Catholic Church in Sarasota, I interviewed four members of the class together. Two of the women said their reasons for joining the Church had to do with a feeling of emptiness. Pat recalled:

> I prayed at night, and I talked to God. But when [mother] died, it turned me off altogether. I thought there was no such thing as God. And it wasn't until two years ago, when my husband and I got back together after a separation of six months, that we realized that there's something else besides people and material things. I had been missing something, but still I didn't go to the Church. Then in July this year I started going back to St. Martha's and began this class. And I realized what was missing. It was God . . . Jesus Christ. I feel better.

A young, hard-working electrical contractor in Searsport, Maine talked of the reason he and his wife joined the local Methodist Church.

> I was tired of the everyday grind. I really felt all along that there was something missing. I went to church as a youth just

about every Sunday. I was in every activity there. I went through boot camp. And then I lost it. I probably didn't go for ten years. And to me there was something missing in my life. I couldn't put my finger on it, even though I tried and tried again. But I knew there was something missing. My children started going to Sunday School, my wife started, and I said, "Maybe this is what I'm missing." So I tried it, and that's what I was missing.

Nan, a young woman in Sarasota who had rejected her early Catholic training, recalled thinking of herself as an atheist. Through a series of contacts with Christians of different denominations, she was led to The Tabernacle, the large non-denominational congregation that has attracted so many formerly unchurched. Nan told why, "It's hard to put a finger on it. I guess I could just honestly say that I was not fulfilled. I knew that there had to be something more for my life. I knew that there was more than just living and breathing and dying and being buried and turning into fertilizer or something. And the minute I ran into Jesus Christ, I knew that He was the answer. It was just a matter of finding Him. I was 19."

Suzannah, 40, married and obviously well-off, tells of her reasons for seeking church membership in Sarasota, "it seems to me that I was very unhappy. Exterior of my life was pretty good—no financial problems, marriage was okay. I think of it as the brokenness in me, that I was just not happy. And looking back, I think I searched for a long time. . . . There was a lot of upheaval in my life, and I started going to a counselor. I was in therapy for a couple of years." She continued her searching, including reading books about different religions, and considered going off to a Zen monastery for a while. She went instead to a class in Christian meditation. "I would say within the first two weeks it became clear to me that my Baptism was a valid commitment, that Christianity was my way, the way for me. Had a lot of trouble with what it might be for other people, but it was clear that I already had made a commitment."

Kara remembers staying with her childhood Church "until I could skip church without my father yelling at me, which was when

I went to college. I just didn't feel that I needed religion at the time. There were too many other things that I was concerned with." She married a young man of strong Presbyterian faith. Living now in University Village, housing for married students at Michigan State University, Kara observed, "We're just about the only people of all of our friends who even go to church, or go regularly." Why did this young couple swim against the stream? "I think almost I had time, I had room, I had a space that I wanted to fill. ... As I got out of school and got more into a routine and a job and so forth, I felt, 'Well, hey, I have some time, I'm going to fill it up.' " Kara claimed she wanted to learn about the "history of God, and everything, really," to help fill that space.

Nettie joined Calvary Chapel in Orange County partly because of the fellowship, which she terms a "spiritual family." But she said that there was something even before that. "The thing that made me give myself to the Lord was an emptiness inside that I was seeking to fill with different religions, different things, relationships with men. I guess my conversion was just all of a sudden realizing who I was, a sinner, unclean before God, and who Jesus was with the ability to wash me and save me."

Some described emptiness in terms of loneliness. A reaffiliated member of the Catholic Church in Sarasota said:

> I just reached the point in my life when I discovered a great loneliness, and felt I needed something. You take a big piece of string and spread it out, and it never has an end. I just felt there had to be an end. ... Something was missing from my life, and a new car or a new house wouldn't do it. It was something more than just material. I look forward to coming to church on Sunday. I feel that I am part of the Church now, whereas before, when I was a child, I didn't.

Yvette was brought to Faith "right on my 41st birthday," when a friend talked to her in a corner of the room during the celebration. She thought for a long time before telling me the main thing that brought her to the Church:

I would say the completely lonely feeling I had. It seemed like I'd always been searching for a real friend. When I had friends, I guess I was just overly protective of them. I'd give anything they wanted, and it was just that I wanted true friends to give me like I gave them. Therefore, I ran into a lot of trouble—people using me and abusing my friendship, but then people aren't ready for that. They're not ready for that closeness out there because they don't understand it. And I would say loneliness might have been the greatest thing in me. And at this point I've found the best friend I've had in my life. I don't need anyone anymore, because I got it. I got what I'm looking for. I know now when you start running from the Lord, it will take you right to the pits. So I knew if I ever stopped running and turned around and looked at the Lord, then I would be in. Been a change in my children, because there's a change in me, and I can't begin to tell you about the blessings.

Two young people at the Church of God of Prophecy youth project in Winfield, Alabama talked of their turnabout and their becoming active in the church. Said Diane:

Well, it was a whole lot of reasons . . . little tiny reasons. But at that point in my life I'd been doing a lot of stuff. I got to smoke pot everyday, and I thought that was real peace of mind—I thought that was exactly what I wanted. But then I got bored with it. I mean, I knew that's what everyone else was doing too. Like they all had their own little pacifiers. All of a sudden I realized that life shouldn't be like that. It shouldn't be so shallow—just to be living it every day for a little fling. I wanted something that meant something. I always knew about Christianity—I knew you could live it if you put your mind to it.

Hank, a companion, added:

I just think that's really what everybody's searching for—something that will give their life meaning. I did all kinds of things, trying to get something to experience in my life I could bank on, or something like that. The more things I did, the more I realized it didn't give my life any meaning. Then I turned to God. I always felt that we were just here on earth

—I think there's a song that says we're "dust to the wind"—I always thought we were like that. I thought that Christians thought that too. But the more you study Christianity, the more you realize that Christianity gives a significance and a meaning. We will affect history, but it's more than that. We'll live eternally and what we do matters. We're not just here today and a thousand years from now we'll be gone. We're forever. That's the meaning to our life that everybody is searching for.

Two things strike me as I look at the interviews of those who fall into this category. Nine of the twelve are women and nine of the twelve are from Florida or Alabama. There is no division as far as education or socio-economic level goes—no "bored rich." People in highly personal, individual ways described the emptiness, the God-shaped blank. It was that "something missing" which nudged them along their way toward the Church. A pastor in California offered this analysis:

One of the problems of people in Orange County is alienation—being cut off, a kind of emptiness. Their moorings have been cut off, and they're away from home, the home they knew in the Midwest or the East. The divorce rate here is 60 percent, so an awful lot of the things that were traditionally of value to people no longer hold them. And they don't want a Church that will put them back into the Middle Ages in terms of a belief system, but they want love, support—to know that there is a caring at the center of the universe. And that this caring is articulated through a community. Which is what I think it's all about, what the Church is all about—this articulation of caring.

THE END OF REBELLION

Fifteen interviewees said that their decision to join a Church was made in response to a need to take up a role that had been laid aside, a need to "go home." Their time of rebellion was over, they said. Some could report no dramatic event. But for each there was a return to former values and principles. They remembered childhood training and realized that it was time to get back. Almost half of these respondents had been Catholics and returned to active participation in their Church. The remainder represented eight different denominations. Almost all had an "in-out-in" experience with the same Church in which they had been raised. The appropriate image is a closing circle. Some claimed that they were violently anti-Church for a period. Others said that although they left the Church they had never left Christ. Jimmy, a member of the Free Will Baptist Church in Alabama, recalls his early training:

> When I was young and went to church, I went because I was made to. But if the teacher was teaching the Word, I'd get something out of it. I always did, even if I went with the wrong attitude. Just some of the simplest things sometimes stick with you. In my teens I had a really good Sunday School teacher. She was the type that was really interested in kids and really loved them . . . and you could tell. Even though I didn't care about going to Sunday School, I went anyhow. Even though I didn't get saved at the time, I learned a few principles that stuck with me. If I hadn't of gone, I would never have known that I should be saved. I did know what I ought to do. I just didn't do it. Even though I'd been out of the Church for 20 years, I always thought about it, because I reckon that's how I've been raised. . . . That's what I was saying the other night. It's real important for a teacher to teach the Word when they got pretty young children in their classes. I'm talking about from two years on up. If they have any understanding at all of what you're trying to teach them, it'll stay with them. It might make the difference for them of being saved or not when they get older. I don't know how it is everywhere else, but everywhere I've been, when kids get to be 18-19, they just kind of drop out.

Down in Nokomis, Florida Dawn found herself pretty much alone, having moved away from her home and family up North and her Episcopal church there. About 25 years of age, she was working full-time giving day care to an older person. The Methodist minister came to call on her patient, and Dawn talked with him. "When I left home, I was all mixed up . . . had problems. I just couldn't cope. Then I said, 'Well, hey, I'd better get in the swing of it and get back in, into getting some more needed faith.' [The church] is a place where you can really go and just meditate and work out your little problems."

Kirk joined the Christian Reformed Church at about the age of 20. He explained why, "I'd finally exhausted my time of not wanting to see those people and not wanting to be part of what I'd been a part of for so many years. I'd just kind of worn that out, and I was ready to come back. And it was about the same time that I started heading home once in a while for dinner. I'd see my parents a little more. So it was about the same time that everything kind of fell back together as far as going to church."

Kenna, a young woman, recently divorced, works in public relations. She rejoined the Lutheran Church when she moved to New York City. She tried to explain her decision to unchurched friends, how good feelings connected with her earlier experience in the Church flowed back into her consciousness. "What I said to them was, 'It's very important to me. I've been through a lot of turmoil throughout my life, and I've done a lot of thinking about it, and I know what I need. I need to belong to a Church, and I like this church, and want to be a member here.' " She attended a local congregational service "out of a clear blue sky," she said. "And I was so elated to be there, I cried throughout the whole service. It was a beautiful service, it was joyous. It was like being in heaven."

Joe, a widower, lives in a pleasant house in Oregon with lots of ground around it, where he carefully cultivates fruits and vegetables. His wife was previously divorced, and therefore he felt that they could not belong to the Catholic Church. I asked him how he felt about the Church while he wasn't attending. Here is his answer:

Before I was married, had I missed Mass on Sunday, that hurt me real bad. I couldn't wait until confession to get that off my mind. Later on, when I started drifting away, that didn't bother me. You get into this feeling that nothing matters. You make yourself believe that you are living a good Christian life, even though you are not following the laws of the Church. You're not killing anybody, are not stealing, so everything is fine. You continue on in that mode of life. You make yourself believe that this is okay.

Joe attended sporadically without his wife. The changes in the Catholic Church hit him hard. "I felt the people were losing their reverence for God and everything else, the way this new Mass was coming along. Some of the new priests seemed kind of 'mod.' I met a priest that I knew walking down the street. Good thing that I did know him; he had raised a beard and he had on one of these Hawaiian shirts. I had always seen a priest with a black suit and collar. It took me a long time to get used to the new image."

After his wife died, Joe realized that there would have been help to resolve their marriage problem had he investigated further. "I always lived in hope that maybe her former husband would go first and we could solve our problems, but it didn't work out that way. The minute she passed away, my stepson was on the phone saying his dad would like to have a death certificate so he could be married to his new wife in church. Maybe we were both sitting there waiting." Thinking about his return to his Church, Joe said, "It makes me feel great. I'm still concerned. Most of my praying is for her, not for myself, and I should be praying for myself too."

Dan was born and reared in the Catholic Church in a southwestern Michigan community. While in the military he began to drink "very heavily, self-destructively." He returned home and attended Mass again "physically, because when you're in that bag, you grab any brownie points you can. I guess it was a perverted sense of 'If he goes to church, he can't be all that bad.'" A friend introduced him to Alcoholics Anonymous and he was given a staunchly Christian sponsor. He remembers, "He talked a lot about Christian principles and the fact that I had a church background, that I knew right from wrong, I knew where to go and what to do. And in the AA program, they very strongly suggest that you renew whatever religious affiliation you had, so it was kind of a natural path back."

Dan now encourages others to whom he is a sponsor in AA "to rejoin their Church when they're ready. The thing that I did not have that I find a lot of people do have, whether they have a drinking problem or not, is that they bought a lot of the fire and brimstone, and they've got an old image of what church was when they were little kids. Like scrubbed ears and 'sit-up-straight.' And they're astounded to go back and find that it has changed. It's a very positive thing, a good thing."

Mim remembers that going to church was mainly "showing that our family was together, when in fact I was never really a part of that family." A divorced teacher living in Fullerton, California, she continued:

> Everything that I saw that went on at church I found boring, dull, irrelevant and distasteful because of what went on even before we got into the church. So in essence what I brought to the church was already so loaded that I could not even get anything out of it, plus the fact that the pastor was very old and very uninteresting. Where I lived most people were very wealthy, with my family being the exception. I'm Indian. I have a tremendous spirit within me that took a long time to reach. It has always been there, but I reached that on my own through psychology. Only by coming back to myself was I able to really realize what my religion was to me, and to be a part at any level of the Church. But without the emotional foundations that I've been able to gather and that hold me together, I could never have realized what I get now with Don Robert [pastor of Christ Presbyterian].

Mim had been out of church for 20 years. "As soon as I left home, I left everything and began everything anew and decided then that I would not take on anything that was not truly me. It was a very frightening thing to go back to something that I detested so as a child through all those other problems."

During her drop-out time, Mim says she was always aware of her religious beliefs and tried to live what she believed. Two years ago she joined the Church. Her psychologist asked her one day, "Mim, are you aware of your strong religious beliefs?" Mim said, "Definitely." As she explained it to me:

A factor was that I was very, very disturbed on Sundays. Sundays used to be just absolutely unbearable. It was a definite need. When he said, "Are you aware of that? I want you to see something, to go some place," I was scared to death because basically I have fought the establishment. I see so much that needs to be changed. He said, "It's going to be all right." I asked, "Are you sure?" I went, and it was instant. At this church they haven't required me to be anything but what I am. Most churches—I have visited a couple since—I have to leave shortly upon entering without any feeling of guilt at all. Because I don't want to be judged by anyone, and I often pick up those feelings from many church people. I don't want to be around people who are bigoted, biased and judgmental of the fact that I perhaps wear levis or go barefoot. I really just do my own thing, and I don't need that.

Betty remembers Mass and parochial school as a child and joining the student parish at her college. "It was membership without the educational component," she says. "And by junior year of college I think I found myself drifting away." The drift continued for ten years. Then, she recalled:

About two or three years ago, I got involved in a psycho-religion seminar. Very small group of people. An old friend of mine, who was also an unchurched Catholic, called me up and said, "Hey, listen, this psych prof does psychology of religion stuff. It might be real interesting." So we joined the seminar, only about five of us. To make a long story short, it turns out that this professor is in reality a born-again Christian, only not the evangelizing sort in her teaching. I read a lot of Jung, which is 'still a favorite of mine. Began reading a variety of authors. Probably my favorite of all is still C. S. Lewis. I feel kinship with him as being sort of the unwilling convert. Something is nipping at my heels. I don't know how happy I am about it, but there's something that needs to be settled.

Betty was attracted to other Churches because of their stand on the ordination of women, but she also remembered all the women "who do remain in the Catholic Church, who don't have ordination offered to them and yet struggle. And the real turning point for me, sadly, was [Pope] Paul's death. I'd never been a particular fan of his, and I found myself surprisingly moved by his death, crying at one point. I thought, 'My goodness, where is this coming from?' And so I went back to a Sunday service at our parish." She reacted negatively to the service and the sermon, and said to God, " 'This is a test, right? You're testing me, I see.' So I thought, 'This is not the church for me.' " Betty went to the Student Parish in East Lansing:

> I was pleasantly surprised and delighted to find that I was welcomed here. Decided a few days later to go to the Sacrament of Reconciliation, which was a very important word for me at that point. I feel I will re-engage to work with women and to find myself, my religious dimension. There are lots of ironies in coming back to a Church. I have chosen the Church which still defies very strongly some principles that I find important. For example, the ordination of women. The Church's stand on homosexuality is an irony for me in that the very people who brought me back to the Church are in fact themselves gay. How do I understand all of that? Golly, it's a multitude of reasons. I feel like God had to use a lot of different devices to get me, and He used them all.

She answered the question about the main thing that brought her back:

> Perhaps a love for the tradition that exists in myself and outside of human foibles and stupidities and cruelty to one another. Because I had a lot of trouble going back to the Church that pulled off the Inquisition, but I'm doing it because I believe that there's something else there besides that and the people who did that. For me it's an institution that struggled for many years to provide people with means of expanding their religious dimension. I doubt that it has succeeded as often as it would like to think, but I also doubt that it's a failure in doing that.

Margaret spent ten years outside the Catholic Church, including those tumultuous 1960's on campus. Looking back on why she returned, she said:

I guess when you have something so familiar, a habit—we used to go to Mass every day for eight years in the morning—it just feels good to maybe escape into childhood or have something familiar. I used to go to tons of different churches. I'd go and never know any of the hymns or never know what was going on, and everything seemed boring and nothing was familiar. I was just so much more comfortable with the familiar—it was more like a family-type thing.

Dave also fell away from his church for a while. He asserted, "I never felt that I lost contact with God. I wasn't aware of God as much as I feel I am now, but I continued praying. There hasn't been a time in my life when I would have confessed that Jesus Christ wasn't the Son of God." David admits that he prayed mostly "when I was down in the pits." But a year and a half before our interview, Dave rejoined the same Lansing Baptist Church on the corner, in an older part of town. Asked why, he replied, "Wanting to, in the first place. I've always had this want to be involved in the Church. I want to go to church. I want to do God's will. I don't want to sin. I don't want to do things that are repulsive to God, or whatever. I want to do what God wants me to do. And I think that was the main drive to get me back to the Church."

Mollie rejoined the Catholic Church after a long "vacation." She recalled:

I had not had any kind of rewarding Christian experience with other people since I'd been a youngster—since I've been about, I would say, ten or eleven. And until I began public high school and started going to CCD [Confraternity of Christian Doctrine], I didn't find the kinds of spiritual food, or whatever, in the worship that was happening in that parish on Sundays. I think I was also going through, because of my background, a big rebellion against authority. Even though the Church was in the process of change at that time—Vatican II was happening and all—there was still so much laid on me under the guise of religion about how I ought to be because that's what's supposed to be done, that I just chucked it. Immediately following my leaving, I think, I went through a guilt phase. Now I think that at one point I still

considered myself Christian. At some point as I grew older I
went through a deistic phase, and that grew into an agnostic
thing, and that grew into an atheistic thing, and then I did
the whole think back again. And before I came back to the
Catholic Church, I spent a year in a Presbyterian community. . . . I felt healed there, and I felt loved there.

After a visit to the Catholic student parish for a course in theology,
she decided to re-enter the Church of her youth. Mollie claimed,
"It was almost like coming home too. Not that it was too familiar
to me, but it was part of who I was, who I am culturally."

When Andrea, another reflective rebel, "hit bottom" there was
no question but to return to the Episcopal Church in which she had
been reared. It was, she said:

because I grew up in that, and I could remember every song I
ever sang, every anthem. But I guess what I find sad about
this is I know a lot of people who have kind of lapsed for the
wrong reasons. I once heard a neat lecture by a Dickens
scholar. One of the most peculiar things about Dickens was
that, having been involved in child labor and ghastly things
working in a blacking factory, all his later life he could never
walk on that street. And the neat thing the lecturer was talking about was the "where we stop growing" sort of thing,
that Dickens, for all his marvelous gifts, had stopped growing
somewhere back there. The question of where people stop
growing, some part of themselves, seems very significant,
and often it has to do with the Church. There are kinds of
regressions people have, but they're trying to deal with the
present, say in matters of religion—with a 15 year-old mind.
That's very sad. And that's why some blanket thing like St.
Mary's saying, "It isn't what you thought it was, we're different now, you're different now, come, see"—is such a neat
thing. Some kind of open invitation, not to pounce, but to invite and discuss and draw someone forward. It's clear to me
there's no other center to things, and the sense of community
is very different even sociologically. My idea about community
has surely been formed by the Church here. I don't think
other communities bind in the same way, or help or feed or
heal or anything like that.

As I noted earlier, this particular kind of pilgrimage traces a circle. Most of these respondents went back to the Church of their youth. Some appreciated the deep sense of tradition or the calling up of past memories and feelings. For others there was a residue of resentment to overcome. But each, in different ways, said that it felt good to "go back home."

THE JOURNEY TOWARD TRUTH

Eleven of the respondents described their spiritual experiences in such a way that they can best be categorized as journeys toward truth. Square one in some of the journeys was a college course in intellectual history, or the chance reading of some Christian author, or intense discussions into the night with some hard-headed Christian apologist. Each respondent in this group pursued the quest with zeal and determination, often in the face of resistance. The observer might protest that these people were approaching religion rationally, intellectually. And it does seem that the social, familial, mystical aspects of the Church were ignored or at least subordinated to solid, logical conviction. Yet some of the interviewees related their experiences with great emotion.

The tapings of conversations which I carried out in New York City were supposed to constitute a practice session or a dry-run, aimed more at sharpening my own skills than providing material for analysis. Yet I was amazed at the articulate, involved stories that came across. I just could not put them on a shelf.

Six of the respondents quoted here claim Manhattan as their turf. Am I exaggerating when I suggest that life in New York demands an exceptionally rigorous evaluation of the evidence for one who is contemplating joining a Christian Church? Those who made that choice described their journeys brightly and with almost a sense of awe and surprise at what happened to them. The other respondents in this category would attest, however, that such an experience was not restricted to the inhabitants of that Hudson River isle.

I interviewed Bonnie, a young woman from a mixed Jewish-Protestant family, in a choir room of a large, old Catholic church on the upper east side of Manhattan. She remembers being brought to a Unitarian church near her home when she was quite young. While she enjoyed the Sunday School sociability, "Religiously all it did was give me a lot of false sophistication, a lot of intellectualism. . . . Half of the time I was bored, half the time I was intrigued. But the general idea was that you should be detoxified ahead of time. You should be provided with excuses for everything, so that if someone should ever open a Bible to you—it was like a shot, a polio shot. You would never get it because you had been innoculated against it." Bonnie made up religions at different stages during her teen years, "Like art was my religion, or nature and so forth. The only experience I'd say I've ever had with real religion was through other people who believed in it. And at very brief times, they'd take me to their church or something, and I'd be very moved by something that went on."

A bright woman, Bonnie had read a lot of literature and poetry, "and it seemed that in poetry and literature, they were trying to take the good, humanistic things that were in religion and reject the bad, mean things that were in it. The authoritarian things and the literal things that were, like, binding their spirits. That's what I tried to do too." When Bonnie showed a friend some of her poetry, "She said something about religion, and I said that I was not religious but spiritual. She said, 'You're very religious, but you'll never admit it.'" Out in the park for lunch one day, Bonnie started writing in her diary:

What if there is a God? Quite intellectually, I was wondering about it. Is there any reason why there shouldn't be one? The minute I just was wondering about it, without any particular prejudice, I got almost a vision. It was like everything got very tall, everything looked very big, all the green got very green, and the blue got very blue, and all the colors got very bright. I was very scared. I said, "I don't know what's going on, but I have a feeling there must be one." So I started writing poems about "Are you there?" and all this kind of thing. That started the whole thing.

Bonnie visited an Episcopal church and was baptized there shortly afterward, but she was attracted by the liturgy and by the charismatic movement in the Catholic Church. "Then when I started trying to go to churches," she noted, "they didn't want to let me in. The churches didn't want to talk with me. I had to batter my way through, every step of the way. It was surprising to me, because people complain that there aren't enough people. And yet when somebody comes and is converted and wants to be instructed, you'd be surprised at the obstacles."

At the time when she was converted, Bonnie's psychotherapist had gone on vacation for three months. Bonnie forced a New Testament on her Orthodox Jewish therapist upon her return. She remembers that "All I would do is talk about Jesus. She didn't know what to think about it in the beginning, but she came out thinking that it was a really good thing. I think that she was a little jealous though, because she was the one who had cured me all this time, and got me out of all these scrapes, and then at the end, God got the glory."

Danielle is a very intelligent, articulate woman who was raised in a Jewish family. She spent several years acting in different theater troupes. I asked her what she thought of the Churches during her childhood. She confided, "They were a sign of nothing but brutality and oppression. But as I was drawn more and more to Christianity, I began to realize that the popular Christianity that I had always heard around me had absolutely nothing to do with Christianity at all." On the change in her religious perception, she commented:

> Oh, it was something that happened over a long period of time. I don't really know why it happened. The Faith tells me that the Holy Spirit does these things, and I really have to agree. I don't know why it suddenly began to seem to me that Christianity, as Christianity in the New Testament, was true. But all of the problems that one is supposed to have with the New Testament I don't have at all. It seems to me to be true. *The New York Times* I have problems with. The New Testament I don't.

She recalled how the movies brought her pictures of Cecil B. DeMille Christianity. "But even with all of that junk in there, the center of it, God sacrificing Himself in that way, I guess that was the first thing that drew me to it. The enormity of that act. That, I think, is still the center of my faith. The fact that that kind of love existed. That's the beginning and the end of it—the cross is the center of the Faith." When I asked Danielle who led her to C. S. Lewis, whom she had praised, she answered, "I'm very intrigued by Shakespeare. I was looking for a book by a man named Wendell Lewis, who writes criticism. I went to the library and I couldn't remember his first name. So I looked through the catalog, and I got to Clive Staples (C. S.) Lewis. It was *Four Loves*. So I took out *Four Loves*, and I read it. Then I read all the rest of his books. So it was an accident, if those things are an accident."

Danielle described her resolve to join the Church as "the first non-emotional decision of my life. I just came to realize that I believed in the divinity of Christ, and believing it, the next logical step was to be baptized. Because that's what the New Testament seems to suggest. So I did it." Recalling those who influenced her, Danielle said: "But you know, the people over the years who influenced me were people whose lives were testimonials to Christ. I think that they would have been staggered had they known that they were signposts on the way to someone's Baptism. I don't think that they ever spoke about religion to me, but they made me question many, many of my previous beliefs."

Danielle had thought about Christianity a long time before thinking about joining a Church. She realized that apart from the Church she had been inventing a religion, and that it ran the danger of being an affectation. She visited a Lutheran church in her neighborhood and felt that the New Testament which she had read was being taught there. "I find the congregation very nourishing, spiritually," she explained:

Having to deal with people within the Church, whom I wouldn't be caught dead dealing with outside of the Church, has also been a good experience. It's been very painful. It's been a part of that death that the New Testament talks about. I find that it's murder to have to really see and cope

with people that drive you through the wall. But I wouldn't
give up the experience. I think this mountain-top religion
is useless and being in a congregation is a good place to at
least start, you know, with the idea that, "Well, if Christ
loves them, I guess I can at least make some small attempt
to deal with them."

Then there's Jack, a young executive. His pastor told me that
this man's time was very scarce, and that I might have a hard
time reaching him in downtown New York. Yet Jack stopped at
my office after work in response to my request for an interview
and graciously gave me all the time I needed. He began:

I've always been basically religious, but not in a church-going
way. I think I've always believed in God. At other times in my
life, going back to my younger days, in periods of stress I
found myself turning to God. But not reading the Bible and
certainly not going to church . . . Knowing that there is a God,
but not giving much thought to Christ. I had, you might say, a
very Judaic way of looking at things, not Christian. But I
thought of myself as a Christian. And that's what really
turned me to the Church—really studying, reading the Bible
and thinking about what Christ means. It was that focus upon
Jesus that was so important to me.

Jack snapped an Achilles tendon and, during that period of in-
activity in a cast, suffered the loss of a younger brother in a
plane crash. His newly-adopted Methodist congregation became a
focal point in his life at this time:

It really held my spirits up when I needed it. It's a sense of
security that I didn't have before, which has really made me
feel a lot less anxious and more open about myself. Another
great thing about the Church, especially in a place like New
York, I have found, is that it gives me a perspective on the
whole spectrum of human experience, from the very small
children on up to the very old people. It's a community that
you just don't find elsewhere. Being a single person in New
York can be such a stratified experience. Singles' bars, playing squash at the Harvard Club, there's the macho scene and
then the single person kind of thing. In Church I've gotten to
know many couples, old and young. . . . And it's a beautiful

thing, that all these people share this value. I think I'm probably unusual in that I had to go in through the Bible. I had to find my way intellectually. I think others could probably be induced to come and get to know people and get involved in activities. And from there, try to get them to go to Bible study and work on them that way. That might be an easier way of doing it. I've always seemed to take the hard way.

Another interviewee, Suzannah, began her search from a feeling of emptiness. She pursued her spiritual journey through counseling and Eastern meditation to a Christian type of prayer-discipline:

In the class we learned a form of meditation and prayer, which is basically an attempt to pray without ceasing, which I don't do very well, but I try. The first goal is to try to pray without ceasing. The second is to have a time of daily silent meditation. The third is to do what needs to be done, and the fourth is to keep a journal. I started the class in January of this year [1978]. We didn't use the Jesus prayer—"Lord Jesus Christ, Son of God, have mercy upon me, a poor sinner"—but used our own prayer. And mine at the time was, "Show me your way, O Lord." I came into the class [at a Sarasota Episcopal church] having reached a kind of intellectual decision that it was probably more likely than not that there was such a thing as a God, based on my cross-cultural surveys of reading. "All right, I think it's possible there just might be this thing." And that's as much faith as I had.

Although her husband had been reared Presbyterian, Suzannah, from a Protestant-Catholic family, said, "I found myself very drawn to the sacramental aspects of the Episcopal Church. I wanted communion."

Bill, a Methodist pastor, invited me to interview him. He reflected upon his pilgrimage from being unchurched to joining a Church and eventually studying for the ministry. "The Sunday School teacher I had—his single most important gift, besides his love for us, was to get us to ask questions. In college, sure you get philosophy. The kids in college are young. We'd laugh about philosophy, but always asking questions. We'd run around the edges of it, deal with ontological questions, methodology and all."

A switch from science to history as his major field drew Bill closer to the core of religious thought. He explained:

> You can't avoid it, you simply cannot; dealing with history, you cannot avoid the religious background of mankind. Not, at least, for every century of the human race up to the present. I was taking a graduate course in European intellectual history, in which you cannot avoid Christian writers. And I read Abelard's *Ethics*, which talks about the condemnation of unbaptized infants. My wife was pregnant, the baby was on the way—those were the elements that made the chemistry work for me. I can't tell you how, except I know God puts His little finger into the stewpot and turns it on. I got to thinking about these people—Abelard, Augustine, Spinoza, Alfred North Whitehead (did you know that Whitehead was a Methodist?)—all these people, some of the best brains that the human race was able to produce, giving their lives to something.... How terrified I was because the thing was turning upside down. That was too earth-shattering—I liked the way things were going on. "What do I want to mess around with this stuff for—this religion stuff?" And I asked the professor, "Did you know that this was going to happen in this class?" He said, "No. I wasn't positive it would, but I suspected it might."

Bill and his wife visited a church nearby. They found that "the whole bunch were so friendly and warm and open. They're still my model of a perfect church, and that's why we're United Methodists."

Sandy, 22, works as a mason and lives with his parents in Belfast, Maine. He remembers thinking in his teens that "it was weak and sick that people couldn't rely on themselves but leaned on God for a crutch." After a severe bout with different drugs, Sandy remembers, he read his first religious book, *The Late, Great Planet Earth*, by Hal Lindsey. (Several other younger respondents also claimed that Lindsey's book was an important event in their religious growth.) Sandy recalled attending a church service with relatives at a military base chapel:

I must have wondered if the chaplain really believed what he was saying. You don't know till after you know the Lord why people would want to tell other people about Him. A short time after that, I took up that book by Harold Lindsey, and I saw the cover, "There's a new world coming," and that it talked about prophecy. I had a hunger for things like that—the future, everyone's interested in the future. This is kind of what started me into believing. . . . I feel the Lord used that, because I had such a hunger to know why I'm here.

Sandy's journey took him to the Southwest to visit relatives, where he suffered a severe psychological disturbance, leading to a time of healing back home. At one point, he remembers:

It seemed like Jesus Christ, His Spirit, just came over me. Like he was using the radio as a medium, a vehicle. Everything that came out of there, it seemed, was Jesus Christ talking to me. . . . I went to bed that night, and it seemed like there was a glow. It seemed like I was blessed, and I knew that I was going to be all right. I just felt at peace with myself. With God, I knew that He wanted me, that He really cared, and that it was Him, not me, that made the choice.

After a moving prayer alone in his backyard in the middle of the night, Sandy felt that the Lord started working in his life. He talked about Grace:

I need to come to Him through Jesus Christ, and not through when *I'm* a real good boy. Because He loves me just as much as He ever did, and it's not because of my works, it's because He loves me. I don't know why. I just have a hunger to keep serving Him. . . . I have a funny feeling that He's going to do something in this area and do something in my life real big. And He's going to help me to really serve Him, and the power of the Holy Spirit will really come alive in this area. I can feel it's like a bomb, ready to go off.

Sandy thinks that the Lord will bless the music which he composes and performs:

They may not like to hear something about God, but if the music is really good—I know it's a little better than the rock groups around—it has to be. If you're going to sing about

Jesus, you got to be better than what they're willing to hear. And I praise God—He's laying songs on my heart. I'm just praying that He will give me some songs that are just beyond anything that has ever been written before. I'm just praying that He will give some Christian songs that will knock people out of their chairs.

Iris told me that she was reared "not to be religious at all." She spoke of an incident in her childhood. In a fit of loneliness, she had wanted her doll to be alive. "I made an experiment. I laid the doll down, thinking that if there was a God, He would surely be able to make the doll animated. I didn't expect too much. You know, if she had just moved half an inch or something, it would have been proof enough for me. But sure enough, she didn't move at all. And that to me was proof that there was no God. So I guess I had pretty much settled the question for myself and I didn't pay any more mind to it."

She said that a change occurred, starting quite intellectually with a "binge" of reading some years ago, "trying to answer the questions that kept getting raised." Living alone in the city after college graduation had been a difficult time, but it allowed time for reading. This caused Iris to be more "open to religion." Then something happened. "I had a very startling dream in which there was Jesus Christ. I guess that was like the seed that got planted. I guess it got planted in fertile ground, and it just sort of broke through."

A friend who had converted to Christianity sent her some literature, including *Moody's Monthly* Bible study and material about Corrie ten Boom. "I tend to want to learn things myself. Intellectually the last thing I'm able to do is to take something on somebody else's word. And if I'd been indoctrinated when I was young, I would have had to cut through that in order to feel religious. I would have had to separate what my teaching was from what I really discovered myself. And there I was, like a clean slate."

She felt free to go to church, she said, like a person who just experiences playing music without being compelled to practice. Iris explained how she made the connection between reading the Bible and Christian material and going to church, "The fact that I wanted to be baptized—that, I guess, was the connection. If you believe that Jesus Christ is the Messiah, you wouldn't consider not being baptized. I think there are a lot of things that happen when you're actively religious. I'm not religious of myself. I think it's a gift."

Paul is a college graduate attending an independent, conservative church in New York. His early training was in a similar Protestant congregation in Illinois. Driven by idealism in high school, Paul remembers being awakened to problems others were having, "This concern for service followed me all the way through. It was good and bad. I think that this concern about humanity drove me away from Christ. Because of what I felt to be hypocrisy in the Church."

After a party with college friends and some heavy drinking, Paul remembers he walked around New York,

just puzzling in my mind. What's missing? What direction should I be taking? Like an inner revelation ... but the problem was I had left the Lord. It hit me—the realization that I had forsaken Him and cut Him off. I just began to weep. And I went down on my knees, crying, as if I knew. The analogy I thought of—you had a real good relationship with a girl, and just told her to go someplace else. And then suddenly woke up and realized that she was the one after all, really the most precious person. And what a big fool you were. In some ways, it was like an awareness—that the Lord was for real, and second, my rejection of Him and how foolish that was.

The following days were like a "snapping" within his brain and a wandering, he remembers. He had to go home to his parents and work there for a while before finishing his education. At his home town church, the pastor introduced to him a young man Paul had known. He had been through drugs and Eastern religions and had finally gotten picked up by a motorcyclist who had shared Christ with him. Paul recalled, "He was very happy to see me, and his face lit up. And this stopped me in my tracks. It was some-

thing that lived, and it was the Spirit of the Lord that came
out of this young brother. It was like Paul talked about the road
to Damascus. It just stopped me. I was literally turned around,
and I left the church crying. I knew that Christ was for real. I
guess I was convinced and became a believer." Paul returned to
New York and to graduate school, eventually joining a small non-
denominational neighborhood church. "It's been a long journey,"
Paul admits:

> God gave me back my sanity instantly, in one sense, but the
> working out of all the problems that led up to the complete
> wipeout, and the damage that it did was significant. In cer-
> tain areas of my life I still need healing and what I would
> still consider deliverance. . . . Corporate Christianity is critical
> to our Christian experience. You can't have the opportunity to
> be with other believers if you're locked away in a prison. But
> for believers who have the opportunity to be with others, it's
> critical. The whole New Testament concerns the Church. To
> live your life apart from other believers, apart from a Church,
> is denying God's plan.

A member of an outreach group in his congregation, Paul looks at
the surging world about him in a place like New York. He sees the
Church needing "body life" more than one-day-a-week attendance. "What Christ is really working for in this particular age
is not great heroes but a corporate witness—Christians who love
one another and yield to one another and share one another's
burdens. . . . And I'm growing up because of my experience with
other Christians—the life we have here."

People today have, on occasion, searched and found. Unlike
many others, these formerly unchurched have followed a circuitous route, starting at different points but finding that the
path to the doors of a Church is part of the journey to truth.

A professor of religion gave his analysis of the new emphasis
on the union of a believer with Christ:

> It's certainly true enough since the Reformation that the
> great stress has been on the death of Jesus, who takes our
> place and suffers for us. I think maybe what we've got to do

is stress the union with Christ, the second, other side of that. And if we do that, then we're close to a new kind of proclamation. But that's difficult to do, because that requires a tiny bit of mysticism, in the sense of—if I'm united with Christ, how do I feel that? How do I sense that? How is that real to me? It has to be a return to a style of prayer and scripture-reading and taking time—that gives me an opportunity to plumb the depths enough to find God there.

THE RESPONSE TO EVANGELISM

There is a renewed interest in evangelism that has arisen almost in direct proportion to the decline in membership in some of the Churches. It is no longer a dirty word. In some denominations evangelism amounts to a new undertaking—as if no one had ever thought of it before. In others, it stems from a renewal of the courage and confidence of past history. Each of the ten interviewees here claims to have been reached through the formal efforts of a congregation that initiated an evangelism thrust within the community.

It was especially interesting to me to find people who claimed that the prayers of the congregation and of people—"I don't know in what monastery," one remarked—were the driving force in their conversion and membership in a Church. For example, Walter, a retired business manager, a member of the Nazarene Church in Dallas, West Virginia said, "The people in that church prayed for me. I believe that's what brought me back. It was people I had no idea of what they were doing—who were praying for me. Because I was at the time a lost soul, gradually killing myself."

Others were susceptible to more direct evangelistic methods. Dorothy, formerly Catholic, had been involved in a number of different Churches. The approach that her sister-in-law used to stabilize her religious life sounds very much like the "Kennedy Method," named after a Presbyterian pastor in Fort Lauderdale, Florida. She related:

My sister-in-law, who was attending Faith Presbyterian Church, asked me at a coffee-klatsch one morning if I knew where I was going when I died. And I said, "No. I hoped that

I would get into purgatory and maybe work my way up to heaven, you know." And she said, "Do you believe in Jesus Christ as the Son of God?" And I said, "Yes." She said, "Well, the Bible says if you believe that, that you go to heaven." And that was too simple for me, and I had to be shown that. So she gave me a Bible, and the Lord gave me pneumonia—I praise God for it, because it gave me an opportunity to be in bed and read the Bible.

Two charismatic believers called upon Dorothy at a later time:

And she invited me to this home meeting, and I said, "All right." I was so afraid that it would be—that I would be on an emotional binge. I didn't want that. I took a Darvon, and a tranquilizer and an aspirin and ate a full breakfast because—like if you drink on an empty stomach. This is carnal reasoning, but this is what was going through my mind. And I went there, and I prayed to the God of Abraham, Isaac and Jacob, "If this is of You, I want it, but if it is not of You, Lord, protect me." And he baptized me in the Holy Spirit with such power.

Eventually Dorothy found a church home at The Tabernacle in Sarasota, Florida, a conservative, evangelical congregation.

Montie and Lynn are members of the Christian Church in Monmouth, Oregon. Montie recalled that when he was courting his wife he attended services off and on. "The congregation has an evangelism program where there's a booklet that we look through, and we go visiting people that have visited our church and present the Gospel in a format that they've laid out for us. Lynn's mother became involved in the program, so we got to hear a lot about it that fall. We were going to church, every now and then, and so we were over to her house one night and a couple of people came over." Lynn admitted that the callers had been forewarned that Montie might be there. Montie continued, "They presented the Gospel and I accepted it. I was baptized a week later." Now, several years later, Montie has a desire to evangelize others. He noted:

We as members of that [congregation] have a responsibility to invite people and to share. When I was going to that church in Dallas, they were always inviting people to come with them. I don't think you see that too much, though Wendell [the pastor] has been encouraging that lately. But you know, just going to your neighbor and inviting them, "Would you come with us?"—they might really appreciate it. I know a lot of people would come if they were just prompted.

I interviewed several people who were reached by the forceful evangelism of St. Matthew Lutheran Church in Holt, Michigan. An older couple, the Landers, told why they first attended church, "They have this evangelist team of three people, who visited us over a few weeks. Then we went to their instruction class." Asked how the congregation happened to pick them, Jim answered, "A lady with whom Rhonda works gave our names to the church. I was ready for somebody to come. I think it has to be the right time. If they'd have come two or three years ago, or five years ago, it might not have done any good." The Landers look forward to attending an evangelism training class themselves. I was surprised because of Jim's partial paralysis and his wife's somewhat heavy foreign accent. But Jim told me, "I have a hard time memorizing things and talking, but I think when the time comes, I'll be able to do it."

Rudy joined the military service shortly after he married Linda. The couple lived in the South and then returned to an older part of Lansing. Rudy said:

Out of feeling the need to keep peace with her parents, we attended church. We thought maybe it would be nicer if we did belong to a Church somewhere. So once in a while we'd make an effort to attend. It wasn't that I really wanted to, I just thought maybe that's what I should do—to keep them happy. Like Linda said, shortly after we visited, some people from the Church came knocking on the door and shared the Gospel with us. And at that point I accepted the Lord.

Rudy concluded, "Because we're in evangelism it's easy to get into a presentation when anybody says anything, no matter what the topic is. It's because of the Church that we can know we have eternal life. That's the actual testimony of the Church."

Twenty-five-year-old Fred works with computers, and recalled for me his attitude as a teen-ager who considered himself "a confirmed atheist and lover of science." He noted that his attitude changed because of a school friend named Paul who "approached me several thousand times." He explained, "Every day in physics class Paul invited me to go to this youth group, and I always said 'No.' I had better things to do. Finally I went, to get him off my back, and I found all these people that were talking about love and children of God and Jesus Christ and the Gospel and things like that. At that time, I was into communism real heavy and Buddhism. These people, I thought, were all messed up so I went back to straighten them out. About six weeks later I became a Christian." He attributed his church relationship to the

> ... persistence and just the faith of Paul. He never gave up on me, no matter how arrogant and no matter how belligerent and how—there were times that he'd ask me questions about science and I'd give him the kind of look like, "My, you're an idiot." And he never gave up, and he still liked me. At the time I thought he liked me because I was intelligent and I'd help him with his physics, when he needed help. But he really loved me a lot and he showed that love, and I appreciate that. And the people at the youth group at the church showed that love too. Their lives were totally different from mine. When I weighed the two situations, I realized that I'd be better off to switch rather than fight.

Laura recalled her rebellion as a teen-ager when, unlike so many in a reverse situation, she would steal out to church in opposition to her unchurched parents. Later she complained that church was not very meaningful and dropped away:

> About three years ago, an evangelism team came to my door. People had come to my door before to talk about their particular religion. I thought I'd talk to these people a few minutes and then I'd send them on their way. But this team was a little different. They didn't talk around the core.

They got right to the core, and after talking for a few minutes they asked me if I knew for sure that if I was to die, I would go to heaven. Well, I said, "Yes." The next question they asked was "What would you say to God if He were to ask you why He should let you into His heaven?" I gave some kind of an answer, but I wanted to send them away. They were really scaring me. They really got to the core, you know. Out of the clear blue sky, one of them looked at me and said, "I've got good news for you—Jesus loves you." And I started to cry. I'd never seen these people before in my life. And I stood there at the door, and I sobbed and I couldn't stop. But I still wouldn't let them in. This all happened at the door. One said to me, "I've helped many people. I know that I can help you too, if you'll just let me come in and talk with you." It was starting to get late; I had to get my children to bed. But I did make an appointment later for her to come back. When she came back, I prayed a prayer of commitment to Jesus, and I just couldn't wait. I was down there at that church every time the door opened.

Now a part of the evangelism team herself, Laura says, "Oh, there is just nothing that brings joy like evangelism work."

Both Bill and Gretha in Orange County had little religious training in their early years. Before he started to church, Bill recalled he hadn't felt a need for it. Like many evangelical churches, Bill and Gretha's congregation, the Assembly of God in Costa Mesa, carries on a bus ministry which picks up children for Sunday School from families that would probably not take the children otherwise. Gretha told me:

We met Clint [the bus driver] and Marie, like Billy said. They came to the door with the bus ministry, picking up children for Sunday School. And we got so to looking forward to seeing Clint and Marie about every two weeks that we waited for them to come, and they stayed a couple of hours. It was hard for us to let them go, because we wanted to talk so much. Finally on February 18, I went to church again for the first time. And that was it. I've been going ever since. . . . It's beautiful. I'm not afraid to think about my kid's future any more, because I know where they're going. And we're truly happy. Because Billy don't drink, like he said. He stopped smoking Easter Sunday. Hasn't had a cigarette. We didn't cuss much but what we did is gone. We don't do that anymore.

Bill is part of the bus ministry himself now. He drives and is training to visit other unchurched parents of Sunday School children.

Steve is a new member of a Guin, Alabama church. He talked about the importance of evangelism. "I know there's a lot of people who don't even associate with Christians. They never go to church. And if we Christians don't talk to them, who will?" He told me of his own experience of being witnessed to:

> When they first started visiting me, I remember this one fella, Delbert. He was a deacon in the church. He came out here and I had a flat, and I was already mad. I was changing a tire. And he just stopped by—I remember he was in an old pickup truck. He said, "We're concerned about you." And I forgot what I said to him, but undoubtedly I cut him off kinda short. But it didn't seem to bother him. He came back. He talked to me again. And it was people that showed that gentle concern about me that got me to looking around. And I knew that I needed something. People like that brought it on. If he'd a got huffy when I gave him that short answer, I'd of said, "Man, I don't want any part of that." But he wasn't. He was sincere about it and he knew how to handle the situation. There's a dramatic change in my life.

That "gentle concern" was a key concept for Steve. Maybe he represents others on the brink, waiting for the right word and deed—waiting for somebody that doesn't give up on a short answer and knows how to "handle the situation."

THE REACTION TO GUILT AND FEAR

Guilt should have been one of the early casualties of the 1970's, the "Me Decade." "Looking out for Number One," "I'm OK— You're OK," seem to be more typical of the day. Who could make any sense out of Psalms 51 or 130 or 139? With all the effort spent trying to wipe out guilt, and the resistance especially of the younger people to anyone "laying a guilt trip on me," how could such a feeling survive?

But expunging guilt by fiat and covering over the heavy words about sin and forgiveness don't necessarily mean that the sense people have about their sin before a righteous God can be dismissed. As one person said, "The cross is the center of the Faith . . . God sacrificing Himself in that way." And somehow that center is connected to the struggle between sin and grace. Six interviewees gave rather intense testimony that joining the Church freed them from a feeling of guilt and insecurity and gave them an assurance of salvation. Two were Catholic, three were from southern conservative congregations, and one was from the evangelistic Lutheran Church in Holt, Michigan.

Dora is a teacher who lives in West Virginia's Boone County. Having renewed her participation in the Catholic parish at Madison, she spoke of her religious experience intelligently and with deep feeling, "I haven't joined because of any tragedy or anything, unless it would be maybe just guilt." Dora said that she appreciated the new ministry by two young priests. For a long while there had been no resident priest. Asked how she felt being part of a small minority in West Virginia, neither Anglo-Saxon nor Protestant, she said:

> My students respond well to me. Even though one may unconsciously say, "Hey! She's a Catholic." But I think that's broken down a little bit. Because they see the person you are and don't focus totally on religion. We learn all these religious things, background, Scripture—but we don't relate them to our daily life. It's not related to the here and now. I think that's probably true of all the Churches. The Catholics are doing more toward changing that. They are saying Jesus is here among us now. We don't have to wait till after we die to discover all these things. There's a new emphasis, that His love is here and we can know God here. I think in this area some church people haven't heard this kind of message. Even in our parish we find it strange.

Wade and Flora live several miles out of Danville, West Virginia on a road that winds by a creek. Small churches can be seen along this road. Sometimes there is just a sign with an arrow pointing up into the hills. Wade claims neither he nor his parents had been brought up in a Church. He attended Sunday School, he says, "But never any encouragement, the call of Jesus, nothing like that." I asked Wade, a solid looking miner of 55, what brought about the change in his religious practices. He explained:

> I guess I saw my needs, and there was a good revival going on. It seemed like God spoke to me, and I accepted Him as my Savior. During this coal strike we had a revival at the church and it lasted about 15 days. We were there every night, through bad weather and all. It was tough during the coal strike, and that revival helped me tremendously in a way spiritually. It used to be the Church—I could take it or leave it. My wife wanted to go to church. I'd say, "Don't try to make me or force me to go—I'll go on my own." But now I finally saw the light, and I said, "It's time for me to make a change. I just hope that I can serve the Lord a little while, like I served the devil a long while.

Flora started back to church before he did. She recalled, "When my dad died, he had lived all his life in sin. Just about a month or so before he died he give his life to the Lord. I went down to the cemetery, and that first visit after he was buried really broke me up. I promised him, though he couldn't hear me, I would meet him. That same night—I had been on my way to Nitro to church when it seemed that the old car just drove me to the cemetery—and so that night I did just what I promised." Flora considered this a rededication of her life, but became dissatisfied with the congregation she had been attending. "I went to bed and I thought about every church then, up and down this creek ... and there are several of them. I was wanting one that had Sunday School rooms where each class could hear what was being said. . . . I named every church up and down this creek, try to think 'which one shall we start?' My husband was leaving it up to me. Just before I dozed off, I happened to think of the Church of God [Holiness] at Ashford, and that didn't leave my mind."

Wade ended the interview by trying to answer the question, "What was the main reason for joining the Church?" "Main thing," he answered, "well, the main thing would be—I don't want to be lost. A home, make heaven my home. And I want to do anything and everything to achieve that goal." Said Flora, "Well, I guess I just saw my lost condition and the way I was living. I wasn't doing anything so bad, I mean real bad. I was just following him [Wade] around doing things I knew I had no business doing. So I just decided that it wasn't worth it."

Laura, in her Guin, Alabama home, admitted that during her years outside the Church, "I wasn't a Christian. I knew I wasn't. Even from early childhood, I knew that I wasn't right with God. There were a lot of times when I asked Jesus to come into my heart, but it was usually in the middle of the night, when I thought of what would happen to me if I died. What if the world ended right now? And I would ask Jesus into my heart. Then the next morning my life would be no different."

Tim was renewed in his Catholic Faith through a Marriage Encounter weekend. He had looked forward to it as a chance to ask a priest about his situation of being remarried after a divorce, "to find out where I stand with the Lord." With some help the situation was resolved over the next two years. "So as we stand right now, everything is hunky-dory, legally and spiritually," he said. But before he "met the Lord that weekend," Tim had spent several years outside the Church. I asked him how he felt about himself then. "Well, I felt as if I was a Christian only because of my Baptism, but I knew that my life was on the road to hell for sure. Not only the divorce, but maybe drugs and alcohol and other things. And I knew that if I died at that time, I was going to hell. That's the way I felt." Now a regular attender at the church in Venice, Florida, Tim said he believes the main thing that brought him back was "prayers of other people and the mercy of the Lord. Well, on my part, and I think it was the Lord's doing, was fear," he added. "Fear of going to hell. But I believed that through the prayers of my parents and relatives and God knows who else somewhere in a monastery, the other Christian people, the Lord put that fear in me and a desire. . . ."

Guy, a 24-year-old member of the Church of God of Prophecy near Brilliant, Alabama, recalled being unhappy under a dominant stepfather. "I kinda blamed God for that," he admitted. "I blamed Him for a lot of things, and I kinda had a grudge." Looking back on his religious experiences, Guy said, "I do believe that God allows things to happen for your benefit." Included among these things was the untimely death of his pastor, which grieved him and also shook him from his religious complacency. He also described his feelings toward unchurched friends:

> I'd tell them that if they could just open their eyes and realize what was going on, like the world and stuff. I could give you a kinda comical description. It's just like a big vacuum cleaner. Everything's being sucked into one place. Eventually the people that don't give their lives to God will go to hell. The Bible bears this out. And we sort of . . . we're so lucky we're able to grab on to something. Keeps us from being sucked in too. Jesus is there, like the rock that won't move.

Ronald told a dramatic story of his conversion and his eventual affiliation with the Free Will Baptist Church in Marion County, Alabama:

> We were having all kind of family feuds. I'd come in late at night drinking and going to sales and all. One night I said, "We need to at least start taking the kids to church"—and I didn't think that I could even be saved. There was a burden on my heart and all. I just mentioned plainly that night we should take the kids—or at least she should—I was gonna get out of that. That week Brother M. came out, and I told him about it. I told him I didn't guess the Lord had a place for me. He showed me some Scripture, explained to me. I accepted the Lord that evening, believing. So I went to church that Sunday and I made public confession and was baptized that night. I can't really believe the Lord has forgiven me.

The main reason he joined the Church, he said, was because "I don't want to go to hell. I want eternal life." Ronald's wife, Lucille, showed the same concern for past wrongs. "I know I did a lot of things displeasing to God. I'd do anything if I could have the life now and go back and rechange it. In fact I'd do anything

the Lord asked me to. I'd give up anything—if He said He didn't
want me to have a family. I'd just do anything."

Such strong feelings of guilt seem to lead to equally strong
feelings of joy and thankfulness when the person becomes assured
of salvation. Lucille said, "Sometimes it's hard to believe that
your slate is wiped clean and you can start over and this is wonderful. We read in the Bible where it explains how Jesus forgives so
that you can start over. And that's so wonderful to read and to
have the assurance that that's really so. What if you couldn't
change or couldn't be forgiven? Because there's no one who can be
perfect and we all make mistakes." Ronald added:

> I tell you, the happiest moment of my life—I still remember
> the night—it wasn't at church at all. We went out on the porch
> and we were just looking up and we prayed to God—both of us
> prayed. I was ready if He would have just come and got me
> and taken me home. Now I don't dread death. We used to be
> scared the plane would go down or something, and I knew I
> was going to hell. That's what was burdening me back inside.
> It does every sinner that way. I'd get half-drunk every time
> I went on a plane. I knew that if the plane went down, I'd go
> to hell. That's a lot of worry on you. We're saved and now
> we can pray, and there's no feeling like that. I never been
> that happy.

A Presbyterian pastor caught some of these themes in his re
marks:

> The Church must approach this feeling of alienation that man
> has—being alienated from his roots, social roots, moral roots,
> also the need man has for community. He's hungry for com-
> munity and he doesn't get it with the old singles' bar idea
> where people want to meet people and they discover that it
> was just a place where alienation is down to a science almost.
> What the world, I think, needs is a place where there's a cele-
> bration of joy. There's enough guilt in the world, enough
> sadness—I think there needs to be some place where people
> are joyous, where life is a gift to be enjoyed, even in pain
> and everything else. I'm coming through like a preacher
> now, but I believe this.

Finally a Catholic priest spoke of his own spiritual renewal. "The basis in reality is that people are finally believing that they're good and they're believing that they're beautiful, and I think we're getting away from the idea that we're depraved, we are weak, and that's the original sin thing. But people are believing in their gut feeling that they're good. . . . Maybe that's just me, what I've come out of, a huge guilt feeling, and I'm beautiful. I found that I'm OK and maybe I'm seeing it in other people."

GOD'S KAIROS

Twelve interviewees described their turning toward the Church as so sudden and unexpected and so difficult to explain that it was "out of the blue," an act of God. Catholic and Protestant charismatics often mentioned their Baptism in the Holy Spirit in these terms. One said, "I just began to be drawn to the Church"; another, "It was God's Holy Spirit that touched my heart." Some spoke of time—*kairos*—"God's time for me." One woman described an experience of hearing God speak—after she had pursued a sophisticated lifestyle in academic circles for 20 years, denying any claim of God or Church. "He picked me up by the scruff of the neck."

God's *kairos* was also seen as a time of fulfillment, after earlier fits and starts toward some Church relationship. One young man in California said that his return to his original church tradition was "like a capsule breaking open. With some people it's going to come apart sooner than in others." There was a conviction that God in His own time brought to fruition the seedlings that may have sprouted, then stalled and waited for the *kairos*—God's appointed time of salvation.

A young couple who now belong to an Assembly of God congregation recalled years spent in Florida when they were outside any church fellowship. Said the husband, "I wasn't ready to quit smoking. I wasn't ready to quit drinking. I wasn't ready to quit living the way I wanted to live. I enjoyed these things too much. We didn't appreciate what we had, and the Lord had been good to us, even though we weren't good to Him. He gave us a lot. He gave us chance after chance. He helped us—gave us the world, but we just took it and abused it." The wife added, "God has been with us for almost 16 years we've been married, but time after time, when He'd help us, we'd ignore Him. We'd think, 'This is the way it is and the way it's going to be.' And we didn't think of it as being God. Time after time He put us back together again, and we just didn't see it was Him. The last time we saw it was Him."

Bertram, a new Pentecostalist in Searsport, Maine, talked about his reluctance to get involved with what he thought was a "holy-roller" congregation. June felt the same way. "It was a hang-up with me. I didn't want to go in the front door, either. I would just go to Sunday School," she admitted. Yet now they are very satisfied with their church relationship. What happened? Bertram explained, "Nothing, really. I think it was God's time for us . . . I really do. Because there's nothing else that I can think of. We seemed to be doing all right. We thought we were fine. We didn't have a need, it was just . . ."

Another young couple in the same congregation described how and why they joined the Searsport church. Olly said, "There wasn't anything that did bring us, you know. When I went, there was no big thing. It was God's Holy Spirit that touched my heart and told me that it was time for me to go. Must have been it, because I had a feeling inside to go and find out. . . . I just thank the Lord that He didn't have to send tragedy or something in our lives to make us really see, because sometimes that's what it takes."

Members of the Nazarene Church in Belfast, Maine, Art and Karla aren't sure where God will lead them next. Art reflected on the future:

As long as I'm helping people, I don't mind. I don't care where I go. I'll go anywhere. If the Lord says go to California, that's where I'm going. Pack up and go. . . . Everybody says we were crazy when we left New Hampshire with two kids and three or four hundred dollars and headed south. We didn't know where we were going. We just knew we were going south. The Lord said, "Go south." At King's Mountain,

North Carolina we stopped. We had only planned on stopping for a couple of days, and during that couple of days we went to church. We walked down into the church that Wednesday evening. There wasn't anybody upstairs. The sanctuary was completely empty. We couldn't hear anybody, but the doors were open. That seemed strange. But we walked down the center aisle, and as we were walking, about halfway down we looked at each other. It was like God was talking to us, saying, "I want to use you two right here," and we knew it. It was that vivid. Just as if you were talking to me, telling me that you were going to use me right here. So we stayed.

That sense of God's *kairos* kept Art and Karla there for a year and a half. The couple then came to Maine. Art told why, "God said, 'Go north.' I bought this old wrecked bus. I had a '57 Chevy engine I had bought while I was down there. And it was a wreck." Art remembers saying, "Lord, where this thing quits, that's where I'm going to stop. So you don't want it to quit until I get to where you want me to go, because where it quits is where we're going to live.' So we made it all the way home."

God's *kairos* is harnessed to natural maturing in the mind of Andrea as she talks about her unchurched friends. "I'd say I have about four friends now who are not in the Church but are inclined that way, and it's a matter of time, partly, because they're maturing. After 40 you get to thinking about things more."

Lee, a mint farmer in Polk County, Oregon, is now an active member of Lutheran congregation in Monmouth. He remembers thinking that he didn't have time for the Church in former years and would always be thinking of other things to do. Lee described the change, "I think there was a turning point in my life about three years ago. My children were getting a little older. It was a fairly rapid set of events. It was a total reevaluation of my life and of what priorities I had. And I think church was just a natural evolution from there on. It wasn't really anything the Church was doing that was getting me interested. It was what was happening within me that was getting me interested in the Church."

I asked Lee if it was a tough decision to come into active membership. He said:

I'd say "no." I'd frankly say it was the Holy Spirit moving inside of me, very natural movements in time. It wasn't my wife or my friends, or what everybody else was doing. In other words, I think it was the Lord leading me rather than anyone else trying to move me. You look around and you see what other people's lifestyles are and you say, "Gee, that person's happy, that person's content. I want a part of that action." So as far as what Church to go to, you can say, "Well, they have an evangelism program, they have all these other neat things, and they go out and they make calls and what-have-you." Well, that takes fruit, but not until the Holy Spirit works within, I think—at least that's my experience.

The pastor had called on Lee before, but to no effect. "The pastor came out several times," Lee remembers, "and several of the elders came out to make calls. As I said, I think that bore fruit later, but . . . at the time, I wasn't ready."

"Until I got saved, I hadn't been to church for 20 years or more." That's what Harold remembers about his life before he joined the Church of God (Holiness) in Ashford, West Virginia. Elaine, his wife, decided to go to revival one evening. Harold recalled, "I didn't want to go—contrary, I wasn't going to go. But I followed her that night for some reason. Because the Lord just said, 'It's time to go.' She didn't even ask me to go. And that was the night that I got saved. Enjoying it ever since. Couldn't find a better life."

Elaine reminded her husband, "Aren't you going to tell him how you felt trapped that night? That was the funny part that he didn't admit." Harold did then tell me:

There was no way out. I was sittin' on the back seat, had a door here and a door there. I could went out either one of them but I didn't know those doors led to the outside. I knew one of them led to the outside, but the other one, I didn't know where that led to. I didn't want to get in one of them rooms and get trapped there. So there wasn't any way out. I wasn't in church long enough to know each door. There wasn't nobody holding me in there but the Lord. He had me in there, and He wasn't going to let me out, till I done something. Really, I don't know why I come to join the Church. Only the Lord seen it was time for me to get in after 55 years being out. He thought it was time to get in, so He just took me in. Glad He did.

Marion is a woman of 40 continuing her education in New York. Although she had been brought up in a Baptist tradition, she fell away from the Church for most of her adult life. "I didn't believe in God, I didn't believe in anything," she admitted. I met her in the basement of a Catholic church in lower Manhattan where she had received instruction for membership. What brought about the change in her religious values? Marion had been told that she must have surgery about a year before, so she went to California where she was hospitalized in a town near where her mother lives. It was a Catholic hospital, and she made friends with one of the nuns. After the operation, she recalled:

I was walking up and down the hall—the way you're supposed to after surgery. It looked like something out of *Catch-22*, seeing all these people pushing their little machines up and down. There was a tremendous number of visitors on the floor that day, and it bothered me. And there was a Catholic chapel there. And I thought, "Well, I'll go and sit in it, because it will be quiet, and no one will bother me in there." And I sat down and looked around, and I said, "This is really tacky." Those hideous, emasculated pictures of Jesus and the little red candles and everything. And I was really doing a trip on the room. And a voice literally spoke to me—literally—it wasn't in my head. And He said, "Love Me and serve this My Church." And I was scared to death. I was terrified.

Marion denied that anything led up to this happening. She claimed that she had received no pain-killing or sleep-inducing drugs:

My mother had the best description of it, when I talked to her about it. She said it was like God picked me up by the scruff of the neck and said, "Shape up. I'm tired of all your nonsense." And I sat there, I don't know how long, kind of stunned. I kind of knew that God was saying, "I'm giving you a chance. And you're so thick-headed, I have to hit you over the head with something to make you see it." And I knew then that I didn't have any choice, and that if I rejected this, I was lost.

Because she was moving to New York in such a short time, Marion postponed beginning any instruction. She said that not that much has changed in her life in the wake of her experience. "I don't know if I feel any different. I don't feel that I have any switched dependencies or anything like that. I wonder sometimes why God chose me, because I'm an imperfect kind of pattern . . . I'll obey the rules. I don't agree with all of them, nevertheless it's kind of a package deal. You can't pick and choose and say this part I like and that part I don't. So I'm saying, 'OK, God, I'm doing what You told me to do, and I'm going to play fair.' " Describing again the main thing that turned her to the Church, Marion elaborated:

God yelling at me, literally. I would never have chosen to join the Catholic Church. I'm causing myself a great deal of problems. I think the only thing harder God could have told me to do would be to become a holy-roller or something like that. That was hard—alien to my background—it was just a hard thing.

Warren came from a highly educated family. Both parents were professors; one was Catholic and the other Protestant. He remembers going to Sunday School at a liberal church. "Between the ages of five and six I began asking myself why I was going. I could only answer myself, 'To learn about God.' Then I got into a questioning at age six, whether I actually believed that there did exist such an entity. I decided 'No,' so that was the last time I went to church for the next 20 years." He articulated his opposition to Christianity in high school, and there soon arose a "Save Warren" club. With some feelings of exhaustion, he put religious questions out of his mind during college. But not for long:

In physiological psychology I was trying to figure out how the brain works, and I simply didn't have any sense that the Church or church people had anything worthwhile to say to me. Then I had a very profound experience which was precipitated by the assassination of Martin Luther King. The day after that event, I set foot in a church for the first time in 20 years, simply to participate in memorial services for Martin Luther King. And I did so every day for the next four or five days. The following Sunday I went to the University Chapel. The preacher was just back from being with King's family and associates. From his sermon I simply had a very profound conversion experience. If you had asked me before that hour if I ever thought that I might possibly come to believe in God or come to believe that Jesus was the Son of God, I would have denied even the possibility.

Communion was being observed that day. Warren recalled that he stood up:

I thought that I was walking out of the building because communion had always been one of the most obscene aspects of Christianity for me. I couldn't even think that I was walking up to the altar, but indeed I was walking up to the altar. There it was. And I was truly eating the body and blood of my Savior, Jesus Christ. That was a very profound moment in my life. So then for the next several weeks I just had to reorganize my entire conceptual system. It was based on premises that did not accept the validity of there being a God or there being a Son of God. After I reorganized it, and began thinking about the bits and pieces of Christianity that I had sort of picked up along the way, I began to understand that it was indeed in the more ancient and specifically the more liturgical approaches to Christianity that there was any communication with God. That was the only way to go.

I asked Warren, now a doctor in New York, what influenced him to think about joining a Church. He explained:

I realized that if I believed in God, there were only very rare occasions in my life when I could communicate directly with Him. And I realized that the Church was what He put on this earth, in order for us to have an appropriate communication with Him on the days when we weren't in ecstatic, transcendent communication with Him. The Church seemed to fit that role precisely. I could go about some daily work and trust the Church to put me into the proper context. Most of my colleagues think I'm crazy to believe "that sort of stuff." They consider this scientific trip they're on *the* search for truth and think that most religious folk are happy to make up the truth or to take up a truth that was made by somebody else hundreds of years ago and are no longer questioning minds. I can talk with them in such a way as to let them believe that one can be a very honest, powerfully penetrating scientist and yet also still believe this. I think that if they actually do see people whom they consider intelligent, honest people, articulating in the rituals of the Church and stating boldly that they do indeed believe these words, and that the elements of this ritual are truly what they say they are, that is the sort of thing which would make them stop and think.

Considering the unmet needs of unchurched intellectuals, Warren has thought of writing Christian apologetics that might speak to people like his colleagues.

At a California retreat center on a Marriage Encounter weekend, Fred and Sherry found themselves encountered by God while quietly writing autobiographical material. "The nuns started practicing their Gregorian chants," recalled Sherry, "and I listened to this, and I just went bananas. At that point I just started writing on religion, and started describing my feelings about it. And it all kind of fell into place."

Now they both teach confirmation class to children in their parish. Fred observed that his teaching of the lessons might not bear immediate fruit. But in an intelligent and persuasive way, he shared his philosophy of teaching—and revealed something of his own faith experience. Here's how it happens, he asserted:

If it's going to be taught, it's going to be taught by living my life the way I live it and showing what I believe. I also believe that somewhere in everybody's life they will come to their own grips with what it is. I can't tell their timetable any more than anybody could have told me what my timetable was. And I guess we tell this to the kids in confirmation class, "But some day you will begin to understand. Some day, whether it's now or in the future. You have the facts, but some day they will begin to mean more to you. Some day you will begin to question more. Don't be afraid of it. Seek out help and try to find a place to open up those questions and explore them." And it's within everybody. It's like a capsule. With some people it's going to open up. But just that faith is very real, and God is very real and He is there. And He will speak to you if you'll just sit and be willing to listen to Him. People used to tell me back in school there is a divine pattern. I never believed any of it, but I can't deny it anymore. It's very much a part of my life. I don't know where it's taking me. I don't know where I'll be in the future. I don't know what the real answer is for me, but I'm still growing along with all these other people who are telling me about faith. But I know it's happening and I know I'm going somewhere. And I guess that's what I feel it's all about, it's growth. You may think that you've reached a plateau, but you haven't. It will open itself up again.

The *kairos* is a moment of opportunity. It is for people in our day the "now" of the redemptive present, as Jesus' call was for the disciples in New Testament days.

CHURCH VISIT, PROGRAM, SPECIAL EVENT, SACRED ACT

For some people who live a secularized life apart from the Church, some public sacred act—the wedding of a friend, a funeral —occasions a breakthrough. It can pull those people, perhaps unwillingly, into a church setting. Some pastors have spoken of the scowls they see on the fringes of a funeral assemblage as the pastor begins the rites, Scripture, prayers, sermon. People didn't choose to be there. They may be emotionally upset. The pastor, probably unknown to most of them, tries to put together the pieces; he tries to represent God. At a wedding good feelings bubble up and the younger friends may be impatient, waiting for the ceremony to end and the reception to begin. Again a pastor says some formal ceremonial words, and perhaps directs some exhortations to all the gathering, not just the principals.

Events like these give some unchurched people a minimal contact with the Christian Gospel. Add Baptisms, Confirmations, and the High Holy Days of the church year when "once-a-year" attenders make special efforts. Also include invitations to special programs, such as Marriage Encounters, and concerts or lectures at the church. These situations are not part of an evangelism program as such, but they do provide an opportunity both casual and social—"would you like to go to church with us?"

Suzannah was attracted to the Episcopal congregation in her community after a friend invited her to attend a class on Christian meditation. The place, the person teaching, and the people in the class prompted Suzannah to visit the church for Sunday service. "One of the things that's very difficult about going into a church is not knowing anybody. To go to a Sunday morning service and then come back out not knowing anyone is extremely difficult. So it was eased for me by a group of people who were in the class, who already belonged there."

Ed and Sarah come from Catholic and Mormon backgrounds. They enrolled a youngster in Garden Grove Community Church pre-school. Sarah reported:

> When we really needed some family counseling, a friend said, "Well, you know, in the Tower they have a whole counseling center. And it's got a Christian ethic with a regular psychologist, psychiatrist, whatever..." What is interesting is a lot of people come who have had a very severe crisis in their life. They may come back, they may not, but sometimes it's kind of a shocker to them when they get right down to the bare principles, and it is, quote, religious. Spiritual, yeah. It didn't sound like it when you were talking about everyday things. But if you keep asking the right questions, you get to the basis.

A Christian wedding carried out at a Catholic retreat house caused Kathryn, a writer, to seek a closer acquaintance with the Church. She recalled:

> I had become very involved in a creative writing group. And I was doing an article on marriage. I'm divorced. A friend of mine who was Catholic was marrying somebody who had been in a Jesuit seminary and now is working with youth. And they had a most unusual wedding. I had received an invitation on the xerox machine. It was a potluck reception. I thought, "What kind of awful affair is this going to be?"

Out of curiosity I went, with a friend of mine, an ex-nun. It was the most amazing experience I think I ever had. There must have been 300 people there. They had a mime group in front of the church before the ceremony. The priest got up during the ceremony—it was very informal—and said, "I want to introduce Karl's mother." I thought, "How dumb!" Usually you sit during the wedding, and nobody knows who anybody is. You sort of make guesses. Everybody was sort of introduced. And during the ceremony various friends had parts, reading or a song or something—a crazy experience. And at the end they had balloons released. It was the most singular event that I had ever seen. Community—meaning an individual's community—interaction, with family, friends, a totally together kind of experience. And it was so apparent that these two people were not only committing themselves to one another but were making a bigger commitment to their family and to their community of friends. I was kind of intrigued. What gives that kind of meaning to somebody's life? I'm not a maudlin, sentimental person, but this was a singular situation that showed me that life can be more than just worrying about yourself or even your immediate family.

What happened from the singular experience? "I guess it wasn't too long after that, that I came down here a couple of months afterwards. And through a friend, I started coming to St. Martha's (Catholic Church in Sarasota)."

Rose was also in the inquiry class at St. Martha's. Her re-entry into the Church began at a different point:

What really brought me toward making a move was the passing of my father. While I knew he was sick, and I knew he was going to die, I was going to the church trying to look for a miracle, that maybe something would happen—this horrid disease would go away. But that didn't work, so I—it was at the service for his funeral that I met Father C. I guess that Father C is one of the reasons why I came back to the Church. It was what he said and the feeling that he transmitted that said he knew I was hurting inside.

Lenore was deeply affected by a funeral service she attended in a country church in Maine:

A very good friend of ours died—he used to own the store down here. George was working. I had to go to his funeral up here in a little church out in Morrill. I think it was Methodist. I don't know, it was just something that he said. To this day I don't know what it really—what it was. And I came back and read the scriptures that he gave, and a couple of weeks later I went over to the Baptist where I had gone before. I just kept going back, looking for something until I found it. It was just something I knew I needed in my life. It's not just—like all of a sudden you die. There's a something beyond that which makes it real to you. There's more out of life than just what we'd been living.

Having dropped out of Sunday School at an early age in Michigan, Paul was reintroduced to the Church by way of the congregationally-sponsored Scout troop.

When I was in the Boy Scouts, I was introduced to the Church again. The only reason for that was because our scout troop was affiliated with St. Matthew (Lutheran Church). I fought it all the way. I didn't want anything to do with the church . . . and then they say for Star Scout you have to do something religious. And then I was working on my Eagle Scout and they said, "All right, Paul, either you get some religious background or you're out of the troop." I finally decided to go with my scout-master's son, who was a member of the Church and he was going through catechism. He invited me to catechism class, and I didn't know anything. I didn't know what catechism was or anything. It was on Tuesday after school. And everything that was being said there, everything that was being taught there just kind of made sense to me. It just kind of fit together in how I pictured God as being, and it interested me so I stuck with it. I didn't have any real conversion date, nothing that I could go back to and say I accepted Christ here. It was just a gradual thing. As I went through Confirmation, it fell into place.

Naomi was surprised to find that a weekend skiing group turned out to be made up of young people who belonged to evangelical congregations. Here is the way she describes it:

I was planning to go skiing up in Gatlinburg, Tennessee over the holidays. A couple of girlfriends and I were getting together on this. And as fate would have it, a couple of my girlfriends bombed out at the last minute, and I was pretty—I was planning on it so I kind of thought I'd go by myself. But some friends of my parents told me about some kids in Bradenton (Florida), a group of kids who were going up to Gatlinburg for a week, and that I could go with them and get a group rate and all this kind of stuff. There were kids my age, they told me. At the time I was so far down, I had no idea that they were Christians or anything.

She recalls a meeting, making preparations for the weekend:

I don't particularly remember seeking for anything, or I wasn't down and out. I was just having a good time, and I met these people. And one lady in particular just—I kind of got off in the corner talking to her, and she was just so sweet and gentle and so understanding that by the time I left I was crying all over the place. She was so nice to me—something genuine. So when I got there I got involved with some of the kids and they were just so much fun. And a few days went by, and I got to talking with another girl when I was up there, and she shared with me her conversion. And she was just so full of what I wanted in life—what everyone wants—genuine peace and happiness and life. Where I was coming from, I didn't see that very often. And it really turned me on.

One of the girls from the weekend invited Naomi to Sarasota's Tabernacle, which she eventually joined.

Rod and Diane dropped out of the Church during their college years, visiting only at Christmas and Easter. Rod tried to explain why:

I think it was just basically because it was not doing anything for me. I believed in God, really, but was not motivated to come back to church. There was nothing there. Diane and I would kind of wander around from church to church and kept saying, "Gee, a church should be more fun than what it was." We didn't think it was fun or really enjoyable to go. We heard about Garden Grove (Community Church), and we heard about the different facility that they had there. And out of curiosity—I'd never seen a drive-in type church—we went. And it's funny, it's like when you try on a pair of shoes, and they fit and they're super comfortable; you know right away those are the ones you want. We knew this same thing with the church when we walked in because we just really enjoyed going and I feel like I lack something if I don't go to church on Sunday.

Bertram and June were first introduced to the Searsport Full Gospel Church in Waldo County, Maine through a special concert. June said, "They were going to have some special singers down here to the Full Gospel Church, and one of my friends and I decided we'd go." The singers got "froze over somewhere. They didn't come." But she liked the peppy music at the church and continued to attend, bringing her family with her.

A chance attendance at church, perhaps while visiting relatives or friends, brought a new dimension to some people's religious thinking. A young man who had "got out of church by the time I was thirteen," returned from the marines. He tells of his first visit to the Church he eventually joined:

My sister and her husband invited me to come to the Church of God. They're known for being more fervent and more serious with God than some others are. When I went to church the first time, I noticed that there'd be people out in the congregation saying "Amen" and "Hallelujah" once in a while. After church was over, I'd see a woman walk over to another woman and say, "I love you," and "I appreciate you," and they'd hug one another's neck. And it got to my mind right then, but I walked out and said, "That's not what religion's supposed to be about. It's supposed to be a very serious, quiet, discreet, 'in order' thing."

A retired couple in Florida visited their daughter in Oklahoma City where she and her family had joined a Baptist church. When they attended service with their daughter, they both responded to the altar call. For Gil, this ended many years of non-attendance. In Florida they both settled on the Methodist Church and now attend regularly.

Wade owns a gasoline station in Costa, West Virginia. His father was an Adventist minister, but they left the denomination. "The Adventist Church was strict," asserted Wade, "but like a lot of the other Churches they got more lax as the years went by. And that's the reason we went to the Holiness Church. We weren't saved at the time we started going to the church. Her niece invited us to Sunday School. We went to Sunday School and we liked the church, the rules, the basic thing, the way the people lived. It seemed like they really lived their religion."

A highly independent thinking man in Oregon was dissatisfied with the churches he had attended and stopped going, until some church publications found their way to him. Will, a general contractor in his sixties, said:

> Another friend gave me some literature of the United Presbyterian Church—national literature. I thought that I had my own opinion of the Presbyterian Church, but this literature I read really impressed me, so I started going to church. I just went for a couple of years and finally joined. Joining the Church was a hard thing to do, it was a real conflict. Because I felt I was joining the Church as a babe . . . The statements and vows I had to make to join the Church meant that I was supposedly a full-fledged Christian. It was a conflict to make that statement, but the only way to get into the Church was to do it. I hope I never get to the point where I think I've got it made. Because then there is no place to go. That's the way I look at it. I feel that it should be a learning process as long as I live . . . that I haven't got all the answers.

Because of his interest in discussion, Will enjoys attending a class more than the formal church service. As he described his contributions to the Bible class, his vigorous defense of certain positions, it seemed to me that he is still deeply engaged in the learning process.

Almost 20 interviewees claimed that when they went to visit a church for special occasions, or were brought into some church program, they felt called to a deeper awareness, reflection or self-examination than they had expected. They were brought into the range of the Church's message. Perhaps most people escape un-scathed—those I interviewed were touched.

THE INFLUENCE OF PASTORS

What special role do the clergy play in outreach to the unchurched community? For 12 interviewees, the clergy were crucial in draw-ing them into a congregational relationship. As we have seen so far, the people of the church or friends and relatives are the most frequent source of evangelization. One person commented, how-ever, that after leaving college he could find no one in his circle of friends who could discuss religious questions or doubts. The clergy may be uniquely placed to reach people like this.

They can also help to ensure that new church members perse-vere in their commitment. A number of formerly unchurched peo-ple reported that they drifted away from certain friends after joining a Church. Their conversion chilled or intimidated some individuals. And those who joined conservative, strict congrega-tions came to disapprove of the forms of entertainment they had shared with friends. Temporarily isolated, these people need a pastor's special attention.

The Presbyterian pastor in Orgas, West Virginia took as a major thrust of his ministry the visiting of all patients in the local hospitals. With many of his neighboring pastors being bi-vocational, Harry Palmer felt a calling to this specialized work. Maureen remembers the pastor's first visit, "I was down there at the hospital, I guess, about ready to die. And Rev. Palmer came and started talking to me. He came down there to see me. And I started praying, and he started praying for me. They gave me up to die. So he said, 'Are you going to church?' And I said, 'Yes, sir, if I can get out of this hospital.' And I got out. And I've been going when I can."

Velma recalled the Methodist pastor in Hackleburg, Alabama calling during a time of family bereavement. "My mother-in-law died, and I was pregnant with Amy at the time. And this minister who never had met me came to the house. And the minister at the church where we were going just ignored us. And that kind of hurt. So then I came up to the church of the minister who visited us, and it put me in mind of my home church—even almost to the structure. And I just felt at home."

A member of a small Presbyterian church in Lansing said, "Lee (the pastor) came over one night and talked to me. I could relate to him real well, and I didn't feel at all pressured or anything. It was a good feeling. We talked mostly about what he was going to do in the church and what he wanted to do. And so that kind of sold me on it. I just liked Lee very much."

Marie appreciated the visit of the Catholic priest when she was spending almost all her time with her child in the local hospital. "When I was there I said to God, 'Give me some sign. Why is this happening? Why are You doing this?' And Father Pat showed up an awful lot in those days, and he talked an awful lot. He wasn't asking me to come to church or anything, but he was there to comfort, saying, 'This has to happen, you know, have faith,' and all that."

Larry and Krista of Belfast, Maine remember that at a time of family crisis "a Nazarene minister came calling. He said that he would be praying for us in the church." A member of that congregation was working in the hospital where their child died. Krista recalled, "I don't remember talking to her, but she remembered talking to me. She in turn had told the pastor that we had lost a child and that Kevin at one time did come to that Sunday School. Immediately he was right on the ball—fantastic pastor. He was right at the hospital to see me. He was at the home several times. But even back when Kevin didn't go to Sunday School, even before we had the child or anything, he came to our home a couple of times just to call. He went around to every home." Asked why they chose the Nazarene Church, Krista answered, "I guess it's just because they came to us."

When considering which church to choose for her daughter's wedding, a new Florida resident recalled, "I had met Pastor W on an occasion having to do with our association (home-owners' group) in here, and I was very impressed with him." His community involvement gave this Lutheran pastor visibility with those who were new to that area of Florida between Sarasota and Venice.

Ron and Darlene are members of the Lutheran congregation in Monmouth, Oregon. Ron recalled, "I think the pastor was a big reason why we did go. When you were around him you could feel the good feelings from him. He was such a great pastor. He stopped by a couple of times. I never resented him coming out."

Pat, a member of the Baptist congregation in Monmouth, said:

> I met Brad when we played tennis. I didn't know he was a minister or anything. Tennis was the real big thing in my life. We were both students. By the time I found out he was a pastor, it was too late—we were friends. He seemed so full of life; he had a zest for everything. I couldn't associate in my mind what I thought about church people, and especially a minister, with him. I don't mean we rushed off to church. We were having personal problems about then, and after three months I said, "Why don't we go to that church?"

Pat felt some embarrassment with the realization that his tennis partner was a minister. "I didn't know what I had said in front of him. I had an awfully tough mouth at the time," he recalled. "I felt real good the minute I met Brad in the hall again. He came up and shook hands and made me feel that he was glad to see me."

When he was studying at the Oregon College of Education, Stan remembers:

> Wendell [the minister of the First Christian Church] stopped by one night. I went with a friend of mine to church for the heck of it one Sunday. I signed a card, but I had no idea that that meant the minister would call. Sure enough— there he was. We welcomed him in and we talked for a while. It made an impression on myself and Earl, who was one of the fellows. And Wendell stopped by once a week for a long time. We talked and we had some good discussions, but it never sunk in. At the time I was drinking a lot, as an awful lot of college kids do, but it was becoming a problem with me. I was becoming depressed with it. I was just at a crossroad in life, you could say, and Wendell really came at a good time. It really planted, but the roots weren't real firm yet.

Asked what made him choose this particular denomination, he said, "Ah, Wendell mostly. I didn't think of denomination much, except that I really got along with Wendell and he gave me some really good advice. So I just started going to church there."

In Huntington Beach, California, John, a new Lutheran decided to give the Church a chance because of the reputation of the local pastor. He explained:

> I hadn't been to church since—maybe a couple of times here and there. But everybody told me about this pastor and the type of individual he was. And I know him personally and I know him as the pastor, and I like the way he talks. I like what he has to say. I like the importance he puts on certain things. He says he's got friends that don't go to church. Like when things go bad, don't expect church to make everything better. It's just not going to do that. He does things like, "Hey! If you don't want to make it on Sunday, we'll have a Monday church through the summertime. If you want to go places, go to the beach." That to me is a—he's making it available.

I asked Mim why Christ Presbyterian Church in Orange County is unique. She claimed it is the pastor. "It goes beyond his honesty. It goes beyond the suffering he has had. A tremendous amount of suffering. I know more about suffering than just about anything . . . which really means nothing except the identity is there; the empathy is there. He's a very strong father figure for me, because I really did not have one, and at the present level I'm kind of sorry for that because he is father to so many."

In most instances the one-on-one visits by clergy were important milestones in the spiritual journeys that ended in church affiliation. For some, the pastor was an outstanding personality, for others he was just there when needed. Some began a personal friendship. Others were content to have the pastor touch their lives at a turning point.

5

What the Church Means to Those Who Returned

One of the questions I asked was this, "If an unchurched friend asked you 'What does the Church mean to you?' what would you say?" I was surprised at the long pause some people made before they answered. In some cases, they seemed to place themselves in an actual evangelizing situation; they strove to give an accurate answer as if a friend's faith were indeed dependent upon their responses. Answers ranged from theological reflection on the Body of Christ to some intense expression of appreciation for finding friends, security, a community.

A 35-year-old woman in Sarasota said that the Church means joy, peace, happiness. "I've never been so at peace with myself or had my head together as much as I do now. Going to church is an expression of that. I see my coming to the Eucharist as an expression of my Christianity as well as a maintenance."

May, a renewed Catholic in Lansing, Michigan, admitted that she had had a recent discussion on that very question. "OK, the Church for me is a vehicle for keeping in touch with God. What it means is that I don't feel that my own conscience, all by itself, and my own oneness by myself are enough. To paraphrase Thomas Merton's statement, 'I find myself building up evil walls, and then I don't see God and I don't feel my relationship with Him.' You have to be with other people, and the Church for me is that—being with other people who consciously want that same love." No stranger to other kinds of Churches, May felt compelled to choose a Catholic affiliation. "I thought, for me there's room in the Catholic Church for mystery that I didn't feel in other kinds of worship I took part in and I need that."

Tom, who lives in Venice, Florida, was restored to the Catholic Church after solving a marriage dilemma. He said without hesitation that the Church means

> Life. Jesus Christ here now. Salvation and the kingdom of God. A new life. One must be spiritual. You can be a Christian but you must be spiritual. You must seek the Spirit and His guidance, and then the Church and all of its rules and regulations, no matter which denomination it may be, come alive and it's real. To be a mechanical Catholic or Christian is not where it's at, not at all. . . . And I find that I can get along really super-well with other denominations through the Spirit. That Spirit is alive and the Church is alive, and the Lord's renewing His Church. And I praise the Lord that I'm part of it.

June, a new member of the Pentecostal congregation in Waldo County, Maine, said, "I love it and I know God's real. And that's just proven to me, and it's a way of life that I think we were seeking before but didn't know how to find." June noted that her husband's old buddies can't believe that it's true that the two of them are still going to church regularly. "People are still watching Bertram, they're waiting to see when he's going to stop going to church. And they come into Harry's Bar and ask, 'Is that old Bertram still going to church?' " June assured me that he is.

Mattie, a member of one of the Mennonite churches in Dallas, Oregon, feels part of its close fellowship even though she is not of the same ethnic background as the majority in that congregation. "There's a tremendous amount of love there. . . . It's just a matter of putting forth a little bit. You know, if you love the Lord you're going to want to work for Him. There never was a feeling of not being accepted. Sometimes I think I can't take any more; it just keeps getting better and better. You don't understand; 'Why me?' He's been good to us. He has blessed us."

Others found a sense of security in belonging to a Church. There is something about habit, the circle of support around them, the prayers, even the admonitions and discipline, that has value. There is an expressed conviction that God is real there, and that God's presence also follows through the rest of life.

A member of the Catholic inquiry class at St. Martha's in Sarasota said:

> For some reason I have brought God down to earth instead of just putting Him in the Church. That doesn't mean He is here only when I go to church. I have brought Him into my life. I've always been a very anxious, worried person. But I have found that somewhere in the past few months I have received a sense of well-being, a sense of understanding myself and a balance. Life isn't going to be a disaster area. And tomorrow, if a problem arises . . . I can still say, "Here I am. You can do with me what You want, and I'm going to listen." I'm going to try to have that calm, peaceful feeling that acknowledges that there is someone up there that is listening to me and is taking care of me. He has given me doors that have opened. And they might not have been the most pleasant doors, but I have learned from them.

Veronica, a new member of the Methodist Church in Hackleburg, Alabama, commented, "I know what I want. I want security, I want love—I think that God made us that way. I want hope instead of just nothing to look forward to. I want joy and happiness instead of just defeat. I don't want fear. This life is not all there is—it's not just once around and that's it. The best is yet to come—that's what I want. I want a lot. I'm greedy. And God's given it to me." Previously unchurched people found that Sunday has changed in meaning for them now that they are attending worship services regularly. A number of people, remembering their unchurched days, said, "Sunday used to be just like any other day."

Susan noted the change as she thought about her new Lutheran Church home in Nokomis, Florida. "Somehow you feel closer on a Sunday because you're in His tabernacle, or His church—I don't think there's a better feeling in the world that you can get. If you're troubled or in need—if you're an ill person needing some kind of spiritual and emotional strength—I really feel that that's where you're going to find it."

A go-getting young salesman named John, who lives near East Lansing, Michigan, used to get into arguments with some of the organizers of community sports programs who schedule games for Sunday mornings. He told me:

> Now we've got to find some way of telling them why we'd rather go to church than play softball on Sunday morning. One thing I'd tell them is about this right of mine. It's my right to choose to go to church on Sunday. I also believe it's an educational procedure for myself, because even though I know God, I want to learn more about His world and His people. And I think that sometimes in church I might be able to find somebody else that needs some help from me, and I'd be more than happy to share that.

A member of the Free Will Baptist Church in Guin, Alabama said, "I don't think there is anything that is more enjoyable than going to church on Sunday morning and Sunday night. And the further I'm into it—joined the choir here a couple of weeks ago—the more I'm getting involved, the more I'm enjoying it."

Harold, a 50-year-old miner in Ashford, West Virginia, and his wife Elaine are new members of the Church of God (Holiness). Elaine spoke of what the congregation means to her. "Everything. You got people you can go to and talk to and maybe they would give you advice on how to do different things. There's just no other way. We got some awfully close friends through the church." Harold added, "Just like one big family. You know everybody. They're just there, and talk to one another. Everybody's happy. You know that when you speak to one of them they're going to speak back."

Carlton joined the Guin Church of God just recently. He too talked about the value of church fellowship:

Harmony. You've got friends and you've got something to rely on that's tangible . . . that's on earth. I know God's above, I know the Son's at the right hand of the Father. I believe the Holy Spirit is here to lead and guide us, to be a comforter for us. Nonetheless, on the face of the earth every once in a while you need something you can touch and see and feel. I found that in the Church. When I got burdens I can talk to people that are likeminded, people that I can agree with and that can be a crutch to me—I can lean on them. And when you're down and out, you can go to church and open up your hearts together. God seems to bless people when they get together in the harmony of the Church. I did hear one individual say, "It's like two men in one boat. You got the same goals, the same ideas—you can help one another."

Now a member of Sarasota's Christian Church, Polly was asked by an Episcopal priest several years ago what her church affiliation was. She remembers answering him, perhaps facetiously:

"Darling, I am my church." And he took me very seriously and he thought for a long time and he said, "Well, I suppose for some people that's fine. For me, I need to feel other people. I need to feel their support and love." And he said, "So I just could not do it on my own." I thought of that many times and I thought. "Well, I guess that's exactly true." I remembered the feeling I'd had as a child when Christian Science was practiced in our home, but we never went to church—I didn't have any interaction with this do-it-yourself thing. But I don't feel that you can say that you really feel the loving presence of God if you cannot feel it through His people. And so many times I will feel down, and I'll go to church and there will just be a smile, a little word of encouragement, and to me that's God showing me that He cares. He's using His people to show this to me.

A 30-year-old man who was unchurched through college, then joined the Methodist Church in New England, said this of his congregation:

Fellowship, and I find that up the road. It also means a lot of hard work. It means keep trying, though, a place where you can keep yourself whole and alive. In a nutshell, I don't think you can be a Christian and not go to church. Being a church person and being a Christian are synonymous, by and large. They don't totally overlap, but the burden of proof is on somebody who says they don't overlap at all.

Todd and Ruth had a varied Protestant background but fell away until Marriage Encounter put them into contact with the Lutheran congregation in Lansing, Michigan. Todd is a 40-year-old school counselor who described his church this way, "It means to me relationships, first and foremost. It means opportunities for me to be in an environment of acceptance and love, and it gives me an opportunity to get outside the inhibitions and the rather closed life that I experienced before." Ruth added, "It kind of puts you in touch with yourself—the basics of caring for people and expanding from that." Todd made a final observation, "I think the Word of God means more to me than ever before because I can relate to the Bible and to the various stories and lessons in the Bible. I can apply them to my daily life, but I do that because I am open now. They were always there; I was just closed to them."

Andrea returned to the Episcopal Church of her youth. Her comment, "I've read voluminously, theology and everything, but there is so much to make up for what I missed. It's clear to me there's no other center to things. My idea about community has surely been formed by the church here. I don't think that other communities bind in the same way, or help or feed or heal or anything like that."

Some previously unchurched people described their feeling about the Church simply as a sense that "God is there." A teacher, Dora, belongs to a little Catholic parish in Madison, West Virginia. She said:

Church for me is real—I experience a sense of joy, of relaxation, a kind of refueling up. Whether people are there or not, it doesn't make any difference. I can just go into it this afternoon; I'll bring the flowers, and I can feel this immediately. I guess I feel like that's where God is. And at least I can see Him more so there than I could, say, in the public school. And I feel I'm professing my faith. And by going to Mass then, I'm proclaiming to others that I'm a Christian.

Sally, from a different perspective, talked about what the weekly communion service offered in Sarasota's Metropolitan Community Church means to her. "I love it. The more I get of it, the more I want, because I'm communing with God. I'm only human. And I'm really talking with God. The communion service itself is the highlight to me. I commune with God all day long, every day, seven days a week. When I get up there and I take communion, the elements are for me the sacrificial lamb."

Patty, living in an above-average home in Orange County, had discussed this very question with a group of friends. She tried to explain how important to her was the reassurance in group worship:

> My friend said that his feeling was that you could be a Christian without going to church, which I believe too. But I said that going to church gave me something, a reassurance that I am a Christian. I need to be reassured. It's kind of like a little kid saying, "Can we go to the zoo next Friday?" And you're constantly saying, "Yes, we can." I need to go to church. I need that reassurance that the guilts that I have are not all encompassing in my life, and the reassurance that I'm at least on the right track.

Two young members of Calvary Chapel answered the question enthusiastically. Said Jan, "Calvary's where I learned it all, about my Christian walk. It's the basis of my teaching; it taught me how to get into the Word. Because every place else you get tied up in works and in bondage and in membership, denominations and everything else. And here you're so free. I think that's the way the Lord wants us to be." Tom added, "Just the emphasis of giving in to the Word of God . . . and that's all they emphasize around here. And you don't have to become a member or sign a paper . . . don't put any trips on people—do this, do that."

Two families who joined the Catholic Church talked about their need for the discipline which the Church placed upon them. Thelma, in Huntington Beach, California said:

> So we joined the Church, and we're really glad that we did. It kind of put our lives in the right mold, the right frame. I felt that I had lived a pretty good life and wasn't really bad. I didn't do things that I felt were morally wrong. But I think by having joined the Church and coming into an organized religion and having to go to church every Sunday—the Catholic Church is one of the few that says it is a sin not to go to church, and I really approve of that—I am made to sit there and to think about it for that one hour a week. When I'm busy, as with the three kids now, that's one hour that really counts in my life. I really need it.

Jim, a 40-year-old fireman, and his wife, Babs, agreed. They said of their new fellowship within a Catholic congregation in Lansing, Michigan, "We both felt that the Catholic Church gave us the discipline that we ourselves lacked." Babs added, "It's my lifeline. I guess it is a way for me to strengthen my faith. I found out that what you hear from some people when they witness about what God's done in their lives is real. Before that I always thought, 'Hey, these guys are putting me on.' But the Church has strengthened my faith enough so that I can see these real things happening. Prayers are being answered. They are real. And you can be in contact with the Supreme Being. The other thing is the Christian community, because there is love there that goes beyond the clothes you wear or the job you do or the place you live. It's just a really warm, loving feeling." Jim concluded with this comment, "I guess it's knowing that when somebody says, 'We really love you, they mean it. There's just no doubt, no question in your mind that they mean every word of it. And I guess that's nice to know. It's as if Christ Himself was saying it to you."

A number of respondents wanted to make clear that Christ and not the Church was at the heart of their Faith. This point was raised by people in different Churches. Montie, a member of the First Christian Church in Monmouth, Oregon, put it well:

I don't think it's the Church so much that's important. It's a relationship to Christ. I don't like to use the Church as a substitute for that relationship. That's where it should begin . . . to help unchurched people to see that the answer is in that one Person alone. If you get that, then by going to church you are learning to experience fellowship and you're taught. You're able to grow then and mature as a Christian. I don't like to look at Christianity as a religion so much as a relationship.

Lou, a resident of Waldo County, found a church home after many years of looking around:

You just kind of go through life. But you're always at loose ends until you have a true church affiliation. You need that constant contact with people, the same moral ideals, I would say, in this day and age. I believe it's essential for children, with all that's going on for them. I'm not talking about hiding from life. I'm just saying—it's tough enough going through childhood. But if you have someone who shares your ideas, instead of knocking them down all the time, at least you can pick each other up. It's just essential to my life. It's a necessity, not an option.

Charmaine finds it easy to talk about her renewed church membership. "I can tell them some of the things that have made me feel good, some of the hours of enjoyment that I've had because of it and because I've actively done more thinking about being a Christian than I did before I went back to church. Sunday has a tendency to tide you over through Thursday, at least." Maybe Charmaine mentioned that weekday because on Friday mornings she participates regularly in a breakfast with ten to fifteen other members of the Resurrection Lutheran congregation in Huntington Beach, California.

Gerry was a slow talker in the group of young people gathered in a Christian coffeehouse. But he wanted to speak about his newly-found membership in the Church of God of Prophecy in Brilliant, Alabama. His comment:

The Church means a whole lot of things to me. It's my life, just like it was for the rest of the [young people who testified in the coffeehouse that evening]. And when I came in, I was real lost—but I found God, and then I found everything. Every time I get to talking about it, I near to cry. I'm near to crying now. I just love this Church. The Church is really my life. Jesus has been good to me. And I don't see why people can walk these streets like they do and not be in church. It just says in that verse—"Verily, verily, you must be born again, receive the Kingdom of God." I'm sure thankful for what He has done for me.

After a heart attack, Ben took early retirement from the police force in Ohio, and he and his second wife moved to Florida. Over the years his wife had belonged to the Catholic Church while Ben stayed home. He said:

Even though I wasn't going to church I would pray to Him, and sometimes when my wife would go to church on Sunday mornings, I would put some records—I have some hymns—on the hi-fi. I would listen to the music, and I would silently pray for a little while. And I thought it helped me. So really I was finally just hungry for religion, you might say. And I'd say there was a conflict in our family with our religions, and not going to church together and not praying together and looking different ways at different things.

When the couple visited relatives, they answered the altar call at a Baptist church. Then they joined the Methodist congregation in North Point, Florida. Ben continued:

The Church is the house of God, and the Church is a teaching place. The Church is a place that can try to straighten you out on many problems that you have, because you have people that you can confer with and get straight answers from instead of a popular answer or something. And it's a house of worship. It tends to—well, you have the old cliche that "those who pray together stay together." I'd say it's the first time in our lives that my wife and I have prayed together. I don't know whether the pressure of the police department was the cause of my heart attack or not, but I really found contentment in the Church.

In describing what the Church meant to them, many respondents talked about change in friendship patterns, in attitudes toward food and drink, tobacco and alcohol. Many imposed restraints on their language, giving up cursing, swearing, dirty jokes. For these people, the Church meant not only fellowship and worship, but subtle (in some cases, abrupt) alterations in behavior.

Rob, now a member of First Christian in Monmouth, Oregon, said, "I'm glad that we talked about this, because I can see just how far He's brought me in three years. Because now there's a really strong stability and there's a complete personality change and everything else. I am constantly astounded at how much the Holy Spirit is working in my life. It astounds me daily. There's just more and more things that keep happening, and most of them are on the inside." Regarding friendship patterns, different experiences were described. Jack, a New York executive, told me, "I find more people that have this common interest than I would have thought. Knowing so many people, my life became focused on the Church, my whole friendship patterns changed and shifted over. I would say that my best friends are in the Church now."

Bill, a 35-year-old contracter in Costa Mesa, California, said of the changed way his friends acted, "People you've worked with have known you for a long time and see a gradual change in your life for the better. Maybe you're driving an old clunker truck, and you're wearing old shagger clothes. You all of a sudden change your way of life—you don't drink anymore, you don't swear anymore, and you don't smoke anymore; your money's going toward a nicer vehicle, nicer clothes." Asked if people had spoken to him about the change in his life, Bill answered, "Yes, they have. They've known me before. They know me now, and they don't say anything, but they watch their language. They try not to swear. They don't tell dirty jokes. They have a little more respect. You can tell the respect they have for you, a little bit deeper. They believe that you believe in your Christian way of life."

Suzannah wondered if her circle of professional friends would accept some of her new values after she joined the Episcopal Church:

I don't drink anymore. I find myself not wanting to do that. I don't go to some of the same kinds of entertainment that I would have gone to. I guess I would think twice about going to a dirty movie. Part of that's just because I'm visible to Christians, and I feel some responsibility to the name I'm carrying. So I'm doing some things that are different. In a year from now, who's to say? But I'd hate to lose them as friends. They're good people. I wouldn't push them out of my life, and I guess I'd try not to make my Christianity such a burden to them. Ideally, having a Christian for a friend should be a neat thing, right?

A member of the Church of God of Prophecy said that, having become an active member, "every day some people try to change my mind about church because they are just like I was before I came to know the Lord personally and before I came to know the Church where people had an everyday experience with the Lord."

Mim talked about wanting to participate in the wider ministry of her Presbyterian congregation. She said:

One of my goals is to get involved in counseling in the church on the encounter level. There are a lot of single people there who have very painful experiences going on, most of which I have already been through and perhaps can be of help with. He [the pastor] opens up in areas that people just don't get into themselves, let alone share with a stranger. He's very much loved. Also the people that are drawn there, people in spaces that are cracked spaces—they're just out there, and he can accept them. Because of where he's at, he or we attract people that are in motion, that are changing, who are not willing, not ready, to commit themselves to space and time, but have to check it out and say, "Oh, yeah!" and they'll be back.

Bertram admits that he tried testing God after his conversion. He said, "There's got to be proof to people that there's reality in going to church." June, his wife recalled:

Well, remember how you had asked the Lord to show you something real? And Rod had got his back healed. And you told him afterwards, "I think I kinda used you, 'cause I wanted to see something real." The Lord had met him and healed him in the bathtub. But it was proof to us that he had been healed, 'cause we had seen the pain in him.

An attitude toward pain and sickness had changed and now these new Christians looked to divine healing as a regular part of coping with headaches and the assorted ills of the day.

Phil, a new Catholic in Lansing, Michigan, said that he has ceased his daily worrying:

> I would say I have peace of mind. I don't worry about the little things anymore, because I know the Lord will take care of those things. I got other things that are more important in my life. I'd say it's given me a sense of direction. It's given us some goals that are good ones, I guess, and that's to be as loving and as friendly and as Christian as you can be, and see Christ in everybody. To recognize that everybody has a little bit of Him. He has answered some pretty heavy requests for prayers, and we're just thoroughly in love with our Faith.

Although he is a devout new member of his congregation, Grant regrets that he has little time for prayer and Bible study. He blamed a longshoreman's work load and the rigorous Maine weather. "When you work, you work anywhere from eight to sometimes sixteen hours. I got work to do around here, and it's seasonal work. You got to work when you've got the weather. You just can't wait for another day, because as long as you put it off, it's that much closer to winter. But I do a lot of praying, even through the day. I pray off and on. Not for myself, but for the salvation of others. I figure I can do my part that way."

Clint and Henriette said their family life has changed since they joined the Searsport Full Gospel Church in Maine. According to Clint, "Our family has been doing things together, more than we did before we started going to church. We were kind of all going our separate ways. When we started going to church it was like a unity, we were closer together as a family." Henriette added that she works "over there every day I have off," and the girls play in the church orchestra, although "they rebel once in a while."

Claiming that her return to the Episcopal Church "did change everything," Andrea said that her artistic output has taken on a new dimension:

I'm a print maker, but that's when the prints really became interesting. And recently carving—I carved for that church. And now I carve on commission for anyone, but churches primarily—I'd rather carve for churches. It has changed everything. It seems to me when you hit bottom, that's when you sort of realize—you're not trying to save face anymore, by going or not going to church, but if there seems to be an answer there to something you're asking, then you go. And it didn't have to do with people—I knew no one there.

Carol admitted that the change in their family life was not all to the good. Her husband rejoined the Baptist Church in Lansing, but she remained outside. For Peter, "I feel good about it. I feel that when I go it makes me more at peace with myself. I see the world as quite a mess." Carol said, "It also has caused some marital strain between us too. He goes, I don't." However, she spoke at length of the good that Peter, a 30-year-old postman, seems to derive from his church membership:

Do you remember how you felt at that time? If you remember, you were disappointed with everything that was around. You were in bad moods all the time, and it seems that it has made you feel better. It's been like a therapy for you, or something. I don't know, but you were hard to get along with at that time. It's like you needed something like that. You were unhappy with your job, nobody did anything right. You might not remember it, but I definitely remember how you used to come home from work thinking everybody was stupid, and everybody had too many dogs.

The thing that snapped Peter out of his overly-critical ways was an invitation to a neighborhood Bible class. "The people down the street seemed to be more humanly interested than other people who didn't go to church, so I decided to give it a try," he recalled.

Sherry rejoined the Catholic Church in Fountain Valley, California. She made some important points about changes that did not occur in her life. She did not have all her questions answered, nor did she submit totally to all the precepts of the Church, she said. Wondering about people who would not join a Church until they had overcome all intellectual problems, she commented:

They cannot find a place where they do not find contradictions. And for some reasons they are not willing to just turn over in faith and accept these things and say, "Hey, there's got to be some give and take." I cannot say that every part of me can be committed to everything that the Catholic Church says I should be. But I've reached a point where I know that I am not un-Catholic. I guess I just consider myself in one of the more progressive movements of the Catholic Church, but that doesn't mean I can't belong.

Some respondents used similes of growth to show their change since they joined a church. Steve, a new Baptist in Alabama, said, "When I became a Christian I was kind of like a baby. I was crawling. And they helped me along. And this church is not one which just forgets about you once you're in. You're on the hook. They will kind of watch over you and kind of direct you in the way that you should go." He tried to get across the same point with another simile. "You plant a little shrub and you nurture that shrub and you feed it fertilizer. And the fertilizer is God's word, and you grow."

Paul described a turning point in his long spiritual journey that finally led him to a small non-denominational congregation in New York. It happened while he was back in his Illinois hometown living with his parents during a break from college:

I woke up one morning, an early job, get there at 7:00, up at 5:30. I just asked the Lord, "Help me to be kind to my parents, and not be so grouchy." I went to work. And coming home I realized that I had not cursed or sworn. It was a miracle—a small miracle. It was a beautiful day, and I had been good to other people. It was an answer to prayer. The whole of my life in the last six years was warring against any faith in God, and in Christ. But in little things, like answers to prayer, my faith kept alive.

Several years after that experience, Paul could say of himself:

> To really give up this self-will—that's something I'm learning through a real experience with other Christians. Not going to a service and then splitting out an hour later, after I stood up and sat down, but living with people who are different from me. I find I'm growing up—29 years old, and I should have grown up ten years ago. And I'm growing up because of my experiences with other Christians—life we have here. As a kid I fought with my brother, but now I'm having to learn how to love my brother. And among the brothers and sisters here we have some tensions. But for Christ, it would be all over. We're learning to love one another and work together and be fruitful together in Christ. I don't know how people grow up in Christ apart from the body.

New church members have felt a strange new wind blowing through their days. It has resulted in feelings of peace and happiness, in an appreciation of Sunday, in saying "no" to old habits, now considered bad ones, and in a different perspective on God, themselves, and other people. A few missed that experience and found things pretty much the same. One or two were disappointed that the tongues of flame didn't appear and church had already become a drag. But most of the respondents felt that an important new chapter in their life had begun.

6

Evangelizing and Being Evangelized

Whether you call it evangelism, outreach, witnessing or sharing the Gospel, the Church has been at the business for a long time. And in our day, after a period of choosing to emphasize other programs at the cost of outreach, Churches seem ready to pick up the tempo again.

Perhaps one of the substantial changes in new evangelism thrusts will be the emphasis placed on "religious autobiography," which may be a new-fashioned phrase for old-fashioned "testimony." One weekday morning at seven I sat at breakfast with 200 men aged 16 to 86 in Calvary Chapel in southern California. It was a time for spontaneous hymn singing, prayer, and testimony— "I" language, claims about what God has done for me. The testimony was particularly striking. It was like a quiet, "Thank You, God," that reflected upon His presence and power. At times there was also a sharing of life's deeper secrets, moving accounts, a baring of soul that can shake one not used to such self-revelation.

On another occasion, I sat with Brian, a Catholic charismatic, in his car in the parking lot next to a modern office building in

Orange County. Brian told me of his spiritual journey and the dramatic changes that occurred in his life just a year ago. He recalled, "I was broken in spirit, my job was taken away from me, my pride. I had no money. I'd come to the end of my rope. I had no place else to turn, I had nobody to help me—except to turn to God. And I had to be broken. I had to come before God and say, 'God, I'm a sinner.' It took me 29 years to realize it. . . . And the only way I was able to do it was through the power of Jesus Christ."

In lower New York, Paul, a member of a small non-denominational church, told me:

> I just split and went to California. A lot of things kept me alive during that period. But in the midst of it I did cry out to God. And He gave me back my sanity. You have to read the 107th Psalm. It talks about one who was locked up in some chains. And that was me . . . one who had rebelled against the word of the Lord. And that person cried out to God, and God delivered him from the darkness and the chains . . . and that was me. I had become a believer—that Jesus had indeed risen from the dead. It's been a long journey.

Maybe one reason these autobiographical accounts seemed surprisingly effortless in their telling was that the respondents had shared their flashbacks of faith before with others, confronting the unchurched, bolstering the wobbly and strengthening fellow pilgrims. Such testimony is not everybody's approach—other interviewees commented that their outreach was quite different. But it is not so rare a phenomenon as many cool, composed, zipped-up Christians might believe.

Harvey Cox in *The Seduction of the Spirit* talks quite a bit about this form of religious conversation. "Autobiography, or 'testimony' [is] the first-person account of the teller's struggles with the gods and the demons. It begins inside the speaker and says, 'This is what happened to me.' Recently neglected, testimony deserves reinstatement as a primary mode of religious discourse. It is a genre which celebrates the unique, the eccentric, and the concrete. It reclaims personal uniqueness in an ara of interchangeability."[1] One California pastor spoke of the breakthrough made by youth involved in the Jesus movement of a few years ago. He says, "Kids were through with the hypocrisy, they were tired of being handed some value system they didn't think much of. . . . And they began to be more bold about what they believed in and what they were against, and they spoke out about it."

Some previously unchurched people talked about outreach in terms of how they might have been contacted more effectively when they were still outside the Church. They also explained how they have taken on the responsibility to reach out to their still unchurched friends. Carlton, now in the Church of God in Guin, Alabama, felt that the Church could have reached him if it had just tried." If someone would have just come and visited me and let me know that the Church had more to offer than I had thought. It's a selfish thing, is what it is. You got to show people that you've got more to offer than what they've already got."

In Fountain Valley, California, Fred, a renewed Catholic, is ambivalent about what approach might have been effective with him when he was outside the Church:

I think even if someone had knocked on my door, I wouldn't have heeded unless they were just tremendously compatible with my own personality and appealed to my own intellectual state or emotional state where I was at; then, only then, I think, it would have made any difference. Where it might have made a difference were those times when I was out of the Church, if you will, and went to a church or to a religious event. If there could have been some more reaching out perhaps at that time, or someone who came up and took a direct interest in me that particular day. In some instances when we were out we would go to an Easter service, or maybe Christmas, something like that. And still there was really nothing there, nobody personally to come up and grab you by the hand and say, "I am so-and-so. What's your name? Let's talk." It might have been a pain in the neck at the time,

---

1. Harvey Cox *The Seduction of the Spirit: The Use and Misuse of People's Religion* (New York: Simon & Schuster, 1973), p. 9. Quoted with permission.

it's really hard to say. On the other hand, it might have made a difference.

When I asked people during an interview how they thought the Church could reach out more effectively, some related their own experience in sharing their faith and told me what they thought would work and what wouldn't. Since these people had themselves been outside, they spoke with a particular, often fervent insight. The most prominent response was, "reach out by example." By this they meant a number of different things. The interviewees spoke of exemplifying the "right life" for those who might be floundering around to find just that; restraining the common carelessnesses of speech (cursing, swearing, gossip); or just radiating a new "glow" that comes from living the Christian life. When unchurched people see something radically different about someone's lifestyle, they may be moved to ask "why?"

Elaine tried to share the fulfillment she has experienced in her new Church. But she cautioned, "I'm learning to be really delicate about other people's search and other people's coming. I'm really low-pressure, and I'm in the milieu of people who are very wary of the Church. I am very open with what's going on with me. The basic thing is just my witness to my friends that it's possible that there's something there." At first Elaine thought she was doing something "terribly daring and terribly different" when she thought about joining the Episcopal Church. She continued:

> The questions I got were, "Now you're not going to start taking the Bible literally so we're going to have to think that way. You're not going to become one of these people who's going to be saved, which is obnoxious." So I had to do a lot of reassuring. This has been going on for nine months or so, and I'm very visible as a Christian. I don't know if they think that I'm weird or not. They notice that I'm doing this, and I spend some energy and not a lot of my time, but some, maintaining my sameness with them. "Hey, you know, I'm a Christian, but I can still laugh at a joke, and I can still talk about something besides the Church," although it's been so exciting for me recently that I tend to go on about it.

Orville and his family are now members of the Catholic parish in Fountain Valley, California. In thinking about the emphasis on evangelism in his church, Orville said, "I'm not aware of anything in our parish that says, 'Get out and talk to your friends.' It's just like Father D speaks all the time of the way you live your life. And I believe that's true because that's what kind of drew us. We saw the way certain people lived their lives and they are still very, very good friends." Asked how he would approach an unchurched friend, he said, "You want to share this with them because you know it's so right. And you know the kind of people they are and how they should be—we shouldn't be saying these words—but how you want this for them so much."

A good friend, Orville said, can be an incentive to him to overcome his admitted reticence. "But I guess I'd have to say what a change I feel it's made in my life," he continued. "The realization that Christ is a personal element, which I didn't believe before." A more casual acquaintance might be scared off by a direct approach. "What you have to do is become their friend and let them know you love them, and they'll see something in you, hopefully, that they want to know better. They'll say, 'Why are you like this? Not that you're a holy Joe, but you love me so much that I can't mistake it. And why do you love me so much, because I feel terrible about myself most of the time?'—a lot of us do. And when you get into that business—I think that's how *we* got hooked." Alice, his wife, concluded, "I think it's just like if you have experienced something yourself, people will see that glow; it's unmistakable. They will ask you, and then that gives you a little wedge that you need to share what is going on in your life."

Another instance of outreach by example was given by Bill, a new member of an evangelical church in Costa Mesa, California:

I think the best way is to set a good example at work, wherever you go, to act like a good Christian. Try to impress people that you are a good Christian without going overboard, without advertising or being obvious. I think you watch your language, show genuine concern if somebody's got a problem. The smallest thing, the smallest detail, you can do to help somebody. If something about religion comes up, just mention where you go to church. I don't think everybody has to go to the Assembly of God.

Jane felt that unchurched people use the hypocrisy of church members as a shield to defend themselves, as she herself had done. She emphasized that Christian people should use the available power of God to live Christian lives. "I think when we really start serving God the way we should, we'll be able to reach out to other people. Let them have the hunger for the Lord. That's the only way they're going to do it. They're going to see, you know. It's like a little baby, who learns by seeing what the adult does. That's how the outside world's going to learn. By seeing us."

Now working as a teacher in the middle school in East Lansing, Michigan, Kirk tries as teacher to share his faith. His friend Chet plans to go to the Christian Reformed Church with him, he says, "because he just about fainted when he found out that I went to church. That I was religious at all. So he's going to go and see, because he said that I'm not that bad, so it must not be that terrible." Another member of the Christian Reformed Church, John, decided to "go easy" with his unchurched friend. He explained, "Lester told us at one time he didn't want to discuss religion in any way. He sees it in us and our actions and our attitudes, and he said that he did not want to be pushed in any way. So that's one person who you don't tell, 'Hey, come on and go to church with me.' But by watching us and seeing us go to church every Sunday and by our actions and our talking and what not, I think he was led to go to church with his wife."

Finally, Linnell made the point that we dare not take on the posture of perfect people. After all, we do live in glass houses, she said. "When people see you and your behavior and attitudes, you may not be perfect, but learning. The thing that impresses most people to try Christ for the better is an example that they've seen set for them through other people who are Christians. Christians should be aware that their responses are being observed."

Another category of responses stressed that outreach is an expression of love, caring, filling deeply felt needs. Troy, a young member of Calvary Chapel, said:

Well my approach would be a little different. I don't think that I would approach them with the Church; I don't even think that I would mention Calvary Chapel. But I would go right to the need in that person's heart—which is love, the knowledge that he can be forgiven for his sins, immediately, right there. Whatever his need would be first. And then if he seemed to be a man who was looking for truth, and he wasn't satisfied with the church he was attending, then I would probably suggest to him to come some particular night to a Bible study. I think that I'm not a go-getter for Calvary Chapel; I'm a go-getter for Jesus. Maybe God would want to use that man within that denomination. But as much as possible, I would seek to identify him with his maker, with the words of Jesus. If he was searching and I could perceive that he was hungry, I'd give him the love of Jesus and the testimony of my own life being changed and of how I was searching just like him. And I've been right where he's at. And show him he needed to meet the Lord. And that the Lord was really what he was searching for.

Clara, a graduate student in psychology at Michigan State University, also stressed the approach of love. She said she was especially sensitive to feelings of resistance:

As soon as a "should" gets attached, most people will resist, especially if they feel guilt about their position. So when I think about trying to approach someone who's unchurched, it's very gently with love and with no demands, because it's really God's work to do.... I'd share a little bit of my own experience and leave it with my friend, because it's her responsibility, and her relationship with God and the Church that has to be resolved. I suppose I'm somewhat anti-evangelistic because I have been evangelized, and it did not have the desired effect on me. It was the people who let me be what I am that had the effect.

Giving physical, material help when needed was singled out as an important part of the caring ministry. For some that is the most important expression of outreach. Herb, a member of the Garden Grove Community Church, admitted that he does not think about outreach very much. When the subject does cross his mind, he frames it in terms of tangible aid. He said, "Outreach is something that I haven't quite figured out. Garden Grove has a 'open door policy' where if people need help, community leaders or anybody else can call and they're right there to help. I know of two families whose houses were burned down at Christmas time, and within 12 hours they were in another house, completely furnished, and clothed. That to me is outreach."

The Mormons in Orange County were often described as reaching out effectively to the community, while maintaining an impressive program for the nurture of their own members. Ed and Sarah (a former Mormon) had recently joined the Garden Grove Community Church. Sarah spoke admiringly of Mormon concern for people's physical well-being:

> They have excellent family-type functions and organizations, and once you are part of them, they really care. They do follow you to the ends of the earth. They want to make sure you're all right. They were here the night of the fire—"Do you need any help? Do you need money? Do you need anything?" I don't even go there. The president of their Woman's Aid called me. They brought clothes for the children, because their clothes were burned. If you have the need, they are right there. And it doesn't matter whether you go or whatever. Of course they wish that you would. But they care.

Dave, a member of the First Christian Church in Huntington Beach, California, spoke of the central role personal relationships play in evangelism. "I think one of the most important things in witnessing is building relationships. Knocking on doors is fine, but I don't communicate a lot of love by knocking on a door. An encyclopedia salesman was there an hour ago, and how does this guy know I have any more love than he had. Building relationships is the most important thing, and Christ demonstrated that."

The importance of prayer was mentioned by people of different denominations. Asked to think about how the Church can reach more effectively, Elaine, an Episcopalian, answered, "Praying for them . . . and encountering the distress of another person, or even sometimes the joy. As I remember to be still, to be quiet, to not lay my agenda, to be empty, then I can hear what they're saying, what's happening with them. And most people are not used to experiencing being listened to. Sometimes that's all they need."

Recommending the experience of church lay close to the heart of outreach for several respondents. Fred, a returned Catholic, claimed that he would come on very easy in conversations with unchurched people, admitting his own feelings in an undemanding way:

> I guess I'd probably tell a friend that deep down inside for a long part of my life, I really felt very comfortable having a relationship with God and with the Church, a relationship where I could be with myself and speak to someone about my own thoughts, and gather strength from that. And if I was to tell this person anything, it would be, "Follow your own thoughts, follow your own convictions." Because I don't really believe you can force anybody to do it. I don't believe you can talk anybody into accepting religion. The only thing I would encourage someone to do is, "Listen to the mood, listen to your feelings, and don't be afraid to embrace them and follow where your feelings lead you, despite what others around you may feel."

Herb, an energetic salesman, thought carefully about how he would approach an unchurched friend. He commented, "I'd say it's something you have to experience. You can't just talk about it. And I'd invite them to go. I wouldn't talk about religion, because most people have had it drilled into them so much that they react to it. It's like selling something else. I'd sell the sizzle, so to speak, instead of selling the steak."

Others share this viewpoint, inviting unchurched friends to attend services with them and letting God work through the worship event. For example, Patty in Orange County said:

> I used to be the type of person that couldn't share religion with people because of embarrassment. You can't say to somebody, "You ought to find Jesus' way." Because they look at you and they think right away you're a Jesus freak. And I don't mean to say it facetiously or anything, but that's how they classify you. But since we've been going to church, I've

taken several friends of mine. One of the boys in there [talking with her husband] says he's an agnostic, but he went and he enjoyed it very much so he went back [to church].

Casual, friendly conversation about his family's church life is the vehicle of outreach for Dale, a Methodist in Maine. "Most of the people that have come into the church in recent years are people that we young people as a group have more or less—I shouldn't say, persuaded—but just talked into at least coming to our church and seeing how they feel about it, how they like it. We don't go out and push it, but somewhere along the line our conversation seems to get to the topic of religion."

Kirk, a new and devout member of his Christian Reformed Church in East Lansing, Michigan, talked with a friend's sister who has "been through the knocks." He wanted her to try church. "So she's going to try it and see, because the answers aren't showing up hardly anywhere else. And I keep telling her that's where they're going to be. I would like them to go to church so they'll be exposed, so they can get the idea. It just might happen that the sermon that's going on that week is going to be something that's going to click. Something they might think got aimed right at them, where they're going to say, 'You know, that's right.' "

Some respondents felt that their own experiences were so fulfilling that they could almost appeal to people's selfishness by saying how much the Church has enriched their lives. Sharing this good feeling makes evangelism an easy job for them. In the words of Polly, a professional musician and new member of the Christian Church in Sarasota, "It's a very selfish thing to go to church in reality. It is selfish, because you're fed there. You're fed with a lot of support and a lot of love." Polly plays the organ in her church. When she and her husband were dubbed the "holy musicians" by their unchurched neighbors, she said she retorted:

"You know, I never thought of myself as holy. Is that what I am because I go to church?" But I suppose someone out of the Church thinks you're putting on, but you're not. I feel sorry for people who don't have a church affiliation. And anyone that tells me that they don't need it, and that they believe and don't need to go to church, I think that's a crock. You can't do it. That's impossible. I would like to ask these same people, "Tell me the hour you pray. Who do you help with this goodness that you feel you're getting for yourself? What good is it doing for anything or anyone?"

Carl wanted to share the conviction he had concerning heaven. He claimed to have surprised chance acquaintances at parties by relating how firmly he holds a hope for heaven and how he doesn't fear death. "Yeah, it's something to look forward to," he remembers saying. "The funeral's not going to be very exciting, so I'll have a good time afterwards."

As a New York City policeman, Tom has opportunities on the job to witness to his faith and the joy of belonging to the Episcopal Church. "I would just say to people that I have experienced a change and a newness of life which allows me to grow and change and that forgives me for what I've been, forgives me today for what I still am. It allows me to continue to change, to develop, to grow, to experience, and to see by keeping my eyes open more about myself. I'm helped to remember, and kept in that position of remembrance." For others who want to reach out, Tom suggested, "If you feel directed to move, move. And then pray that if you've done the wrong thing, you'll be forgiven for it. But don't just sit; move and talk to people and tell them if you feel certain."

Some congregations are geared for evangelism. It may be at or near the center of their concerns. The effort may consist of an active, organized program of recruitment, or it may take the shape of an informal responsibility laid at the feet of each member of the congregation. One Lutheran pastor in Huntington Beach, California emphasized the latter approach. "Outreach should be inherent in the church program or within the people, the community of Faith. It should be inherent to do this, rather than structured and organized. Evangelical thrust is, and should be, inherent in being a partner in this community." His assistant added, "I can think of a number of families who have tested the waters, pulled back, tested a little further, pulled back, and found that because the congregation is accepting of a broad variety of worship styles,

they can find a niche in it. And they don't have to feel like congenital Lutherans to make it here."

Tom, Greek Orthodox before he drifted away, voiced a similar
conviction about how evangelism works. He talked about the outreach of his Episcopalian congregation to the upper East Side of
Manhattan. He sees the need for a strong parish center, and an
enthusiasm that makes people feel good about their membership,
good enough to want to share it:

> I think that what has to happen first is that the memberships
> of the individual parishes have to be ministered to in such a
> way that they feel good in a very real way about their parish
> and about going to church—good enough about it so that the
> people that they come into contact with in their daily lives,
> whether it's in their apartment buildings or their homes or
> their work or their play or whatever, will want to hear about
> it. Not because they're trying to jam it down someone's throat,
> but because they feel good about it. And that very real word
> of mouth, "Come in and enjoy a good time with us," or some-
> thing like that, I think, is one way of building up membership
> within the Churches, and also of getting people to understand
> that a different type of lifestyle is available. People die and
> people change and people move, so the parish family can be-
> come an extension of that real family. And I'm very worship-
> oriented. Without jamming that down people's throats, I
> think that it is worship from which stems everything that
> can help a community to grow. That's where we meet on an
> equal, new level that draws us together and makes us some-
> how begin to seek an understanding that there is something
> that we call Jesus that brings us together and can make us
> brothers and sisters again.

A young member of an evangelical church in Marion County,
Alabama said that the Church needs to present an attractive
image:

> "Get away from the fanaticism that so long plagued the
> Church. Get more toward preaching the Bible rightly divided
> like it ought to be. There was a book, *In His Steps*, which is
> a very popular book about Jesus. Get like this Man. Try to
> be as much like Jesus as you can, and do like Jesus would

have done about the situation. And Jesus would have showed so much love a person wouldn't have turned away, would have had to come back; they would have felt obligated to because of so much love being shown. Young people today are so mixed up. They're searching for something. And "the truth will set you free." And that's just what they want to be—set free.

Others favor an organizational emphasis, setting congregational goals and focusing energies through committees that visit the unchurched. Some of the previously unchurched were reached by just such programs. Pauline remembers the concern that was shown her by members of a Baptist congregation when she was attending college. "What they did was to go two by two to people they knew had problems, rather than going knocking on door after door of people they didn't know. They brought them food and clothing when they needed it. They were there with shoulders to cry on when needed. And that's how they got people into the Church. They cared about them."

Robert spoke of the formal evangelism program that he had once participated in for his Lansing area Baptist church. "We once had a one-week thing where we called on people in the community. I don't think our church grew from that. I think some of our members grew in their own faith. They were scared to death to talk to other people. They were new Christians. They learned a lot."

I interviewed six families from the Lutheran Church in Holt, Michigan, which has a high-powered evangelism program and can show impressive evidence of success. Comments from these people gave some idea of how well the program works. Said the assistant pastor:

About nine years ago the pastor received this training in personal evangelism and began training people on a Tuesday and Thursday. And after they received the training, they became trainers, so to speak, and began training two additional people. Those who were brought in through the witnessing program said, "If someone hadn't taken enough time to come and visit me, I would still be on my way to hell. Because

you took time out of your busy schedule to do this and saw
it as a top priority mission, I hold it as a top priority in my
life too."

Lorna, a young woman who was won over by an evangelistic
team, became active herself in the program. She explained, "Well,
first of all, the Church is the only place where a person can go to
find out about how to get to heaven. It's only in the Church. The
Church—and this is one of our pastor's quotes—'exists for those
who don't belong.' " Ed, a young man recently in college, added,
"My experience with St. Matthew's has been great, and my life
as a Christian has been so much better than my life before. It's
just incomparable. If I had the choice of turning it down or not,
there's no way I'd turn it down." Now active in the youth program, he helps train teenagers to reach out.

The outreach of some congregations is channeled into a friendly
visit, perhaps on the afternoon of the day new people first visit the
church. Whoever fills out a visitor's card may get a call.
Barbara, herself new to the Church, now supervises this program
in a southern California Lutheran congregation. She related, "We
usually tell them that they visited us so we would like to visit
them. I ask them what they thought of the service, how they like
the church. I answer any questions they might have about what
kind of programs we have."

How receptive is the Church when a person finally gets up
enough courage to make a visit, to talk to a minister, or in some
way to give organized religion a chance? Two women who were
involved in an inquiry class at a Florida Catholic parish talked
about the need for openness and concern. Said Betty, "The important thing is that the Church be receptive when somebody sort
of sticks their toe in the water. That is the most important time,
because the person is either, like Rose here, going to mull it
over and eventually make that call or come or initiate some kind
of action, or they're going to be totally turned off, which is almost worse, because it's sort of a rejection." Rose had felt rebuffed when she approached a priest in a different parish. She
remembers, "Even though he listened to me, he still didn't hear

me. I felt that he was putting in his time, but really didn't care about it. When I first met Father C, he spent maybe just ten minutes with me; yet I knew when I left him that here was somebody who had already projected a feeling that said, 'Come back, and I'll listen and I will be there at the right time,' and he projected the right feeling."

Two young women from New York also stressed that the Church should project a welcoming image. Bonnie, remembering how she was pursued by overly-zealous missionaries, suggested that a quiet availability might have been more effective:

Most people have moments when they wonder if the Church might have something. There should be socials for them to come to. There should be people for them to talk to. There should be little courses all over the place that they can come in and sit and listen to, see what they think about it, without committing themselves and without being embarrassed by somebody asking a lot of personal questions. I think it's very hard for people to really believe that God converts people. I mean, He does. God does the job. . . . You should have a place people can come and quietly receive the communion, or commune with God. A place always open for that—not just on Sundays.

Sandy, another New Yorker, agreed, "I guess the only thing the Church can really do is sit by and be ready. I think that the Church has to wait for people to reach out and then snatch on to them quickly."

George E. Sweazey, in *The Church as Evangelist*, sees as a problem lifelong Christians who don't appreciate either their faith or the plight of those outside. "One barrier to evangelism is the failure of many Christians to recognize what Christ can do for life. They take their faith so much for granted that they are not aware of the difference it makes. Most church members are ethnic Christians. They have never experienced the contrast of before and after."[2]

---

2. George E. Sweazey, *The Church as Evangelist* (New York: Harper & Row, 1969), p. ix. Quoted with permission.

Some of the formerly unchurched would agree. Kate, for example, who belongs to a Christian community connected with the Catholic campus parish at Michigan State University, feels that there are still some walls separating the religious establishment from the unchurched world around it. She asserted:

> I think that there tends to be among Christians as a group a condescending attitude toward unchurched people. And I'm speaking of Christians who are active in Christianity. I don't think it's all that conscious. I don't think that anybody would say consciously that they don't believe that the unchurched or the non-churched are as much a part of our spiritual body. But the Christian people I know tend to stick together—communicate only with each other so that they are cut off from other people.

A previously unchurched man of 30, now a Methodist minister, warns of the peril of a Christian congregation's failing to reach out. He said of his own flock:

> Their idea of outreach is just being there. I think they might change if time doesn't catch up to them and eat them up. A lot of people in the Churches are under a mistaken assumption about the guarantee God makes to the Church that it will be there, that it's established forever until the eschaton. They think that that guarantees the survival of their congregation, and that is a mistake. If you start flunking too many of His snap quizzes, He's going to flunk you for the course and shut you down.

Some interviewees remembered ways in which they felt that "the Church let me down" by displaying no interest in them while they were on the outside. A church leader in southern California shared that concern. "I think the clergy have not been out to contact people," he said. "And I'm wondering if it isn't true that we are afraid of people. We're insecure, we don't dare to go to them because we're afraid we're going to be pushed around."

Alice, a member of the Nazarene Church in Belfast, Maine, complained about the lack of zeal for outreach in her congregation. "I don't think people work hard enough. If they were really committed people, I think they would want to organize different groups and really pour themselves out and do things. Right now, what we're doing, more or less, is sitting around and saying, 'We should have more people.' But nobody wants to put the time into doing it."

There may be more reasons why the Church is not successful at evangelism. Sometimes it may simply be because God's time does not coincide with our time. As a member of the Baptist Church in Lansing, George explained how he understands evangelism. "We can't save souls, period. But we can confess Jesus and let God flow through us and control our lives to where we might say the right thing at the right time, to where it would make an impact on another person. I guess that's what the advertising thing is all about, trying to say the right thing at the right time."

Myron had once rejected someone who was trying to witness to him. He pointed out that the Church must choose its witnesses carefully:

I did not see God through the person who tried to [witness]. All I saw was someone who was very immature and very childish using this book [the Bible]. I rejected the whole thing right there because of the way this person was acting. Any time people started talking religion, I would just step back and avoid the conversation. Like this person who tried to reach me, who had problems in his own life. He was sitting there and telling me about my problems when he should have been looking at himself first. Right now, I have a hard time relating. I'm trying to live what I feel and believe. I want my actions to tell a lot of the story. And a lot of people at work realize that right away.

I asked Tim at Calvary Chapel how he would approach someone who didn't feel that he had any need for the Church. His answer was helpful to me and put evangelism in a realistic perspective:

Jesus was sent to preach the Gospel to the meek. When He was before the mob, before Pilate, He didn't stand up and preach the Gospel to them and say, "We should all be forgiven." They were not meek. To me, another word for meek is "teachable," If a person is teachable, if his ears are at

least wanting to hear something, then I'd work with that. . . .
I know that I'm never the one that saves any soul. It's got
to be the work of the Holy Spirit calling a person, wooing
his heart. I just play the mouthpiece. I try to be obedient to
what the Lord tells me, whatever case it is. If that person
isn't ready and God says, "No," don't share with him, just
love him. . . . I believe that *agape* is an actual act of God.

Kirk described his strategy for evangelism and his personal stake
in it:

Usually you think in grand spectrums—you want to do it all
over the place. And I guess I've finally come to the point,
mainly working in the schools. Sure I work with 30 kids at a
time, but I still just affect them one at a time. If I'm helping
them learn to read or teaching them to wrestle or play basket-
ball—whatever I'm doing, it's still one at a time. It's slow.
Maybe I may only run into 20 people that I'll really affect
by the time I'm gone, but that's one at a time. Slowly plod-
ding along.

Paul, an unemployed musician in Lansing, remembers a time
when he needed caring, when he was at loose ends after service
in Vietnam. He related how important Bethel Farm, a Christian
community that reached out until "things just seemed to fall together," was to him. "It's a Christian foundation, a farm out between Grand Ledge and Lansing, 52 acres. It tries to help people
with a godly influence, pointing them to God and Bible reading,
and teaching and fellowship, and helping people. They take in
people that don't have any place to stay, people that are troubled,
and people who just want to stay there and be close to God and
fellowship with Christian people for a while. Basically it's a
temporary thing." In these days when rootless people wander
around the country, I was impressed with this experiment in
Christian outreach to the "whole person."

A very different view of outreach was articulated by Iris, a
new Lutheran in New York. She had a dream just the night before our interview, and interpreted it in terms of God reaching
people even without evangelists. It went something like this:

I'm standing next to a friend of mine. I see falling angels—well, they're not falling, but they're angels and they're beautiful. They're descending from heaven. And I point to my friend and to the angels, and I say, "Look, look!" And instead of looking up and following my hand, my friend looks straight across the horizon and doesn't see anything. So I guess my feeling is more one of humility. Just because I'm seeing things doesn't mean that other people are following that gaze. I guess if I had to talk from my own experience, I'd say it's surrounding you all the time. You would see it if your eyes were open. And I don't feel like I have that much to add to what God is already putting in front of people. If, for some reason, somebody asks about religion, or raises the subject with me, I'm more than happy to talk about it. But that's only if they themselves are open to it.

I talked with Iris about the supposed failure of the Church to get the good news out, this great message which encounters so many obstacles. This was her answer:

But it is out. And it's not necessarily in the Church. I mean, the Church does not have a monopoly. I've been looking at architecture, culture, famous paintings, literature. The word is out. That's the first thing. And maybe— this might sound hard—who knows how the Lord works? Maybe it's important for people to come to the Church as a positive choosing. If everyone were churched on this day, it might be something that would be rendered meaningless. It's only by an act of affirmation. So maybe the fact that some people start out outside the Church isn't a problem.

The previously unchurched remember the attempts that the church made—or failed to make—to reach them. They try not to make the same mistakes that they feel others made toward them. They don't want to be labeled "Jesus freaks," or be identified with a group of overly-eager evangelizers. But in ways tailored to their own perception of what God wants them to do, many take up the task of reaching out. Because of the unique prism through which they see the challenge of reaching the unreached, many of these respondents have been chosen by their congregations to play leadership roles in evangelism programs. By example, by word and deed, they and their Churches are sharing the good news.

7

Implications for the Church

The respondents for this study were all people who had joined Churches. They had chosen to express their religious convictions through participation in an institution. What implications do we find for congregational and denominational leaders in what they have said?

SIGNS OF RENEWED INTEREST

There are some indications of a renewal of interest in the Church. Southern California residents claim that in the last three years it has become easier to speak about church and one's own religious commitment. And observers note an increase in religious participation by young people. Said a salesman in California, "I feel there's a definite swing toward people being more relaxed, talking about religion more today than they ever did. The only reason I can put on it is that they have more belief in it than they ever did before, and they have more of a handle on what they're talking about. The two things you never discussed with an employer or with a client were politics or religion. And today religion is discussed more than politics. Religion is discussed more openly."

As an indication of a religious upswing among MSU students, one Catholic pastor pointed out that the university's volunteer programs have no trouble recruiting young people to read to the blind, to deliver meals to the homebound, and so on. Claiming that today's renewal is rooted in the Jesus movement of a decade ago, a professor in the religion department said he believes that the modern student's religious commitment may be very deep. "The young person has found that by one's self a human being isn't going to do very much, and if he's going to do something he's got to be rooted in our universe. After all, that's what the transcendent God is. These kids are much more apt to be part of a bible study, prayer group or church-attending group than in the small, church-related college I went to back in 1952."

George Gallup Jr., on the basis of his wide background in survey analysis, recently commented, "While the growth in religious interest and activity appears to be across the board in terms of population groups, it is centered largely among young adults, where the sharpest gains are recorded." Part of the reason for Dr. Gallup's optimism is that the recent survey which he conducted on the unchurched American indicates that 74 percent of those who are unchurched want religious education for their children, 45 percent say that they pray once a day or more, and 52 percent report they could see a situation where they could become a "fairly active member of a Church" and would be open to an invitation from the church community.[1]

THE EVANGELICAL SWING

A recent news release from the National Council of Churches states that "the growth of evangelical and Pentecostal Churches and the simultaneous membership decline in mainline Churches has combined to keep membership as a whole relatively stable since 1970."[2]

1. Jackson W. Carroll, Douglas W. Johnson and Martin E. Marty, *Religion in America: 1950 to the Present* (San Francisco: Harper & Row, 1979), p. 114. Quoted with permission.
2. News Release June 13, 1978, announcing the publication of the 1978 edition of the *Yearbook of American and Canadian Churches*, edited by Constant Jacquet.

This indicates that the growth in religious interest and participation has not been uniform. The fastest-growing religious bodies have often been those within the evangelical tradition such as the Assembly of God, the Church of the Nazarene, the Adventist Church, the Churches of God, and independent evangelical congregations. At the same time, as the news release showed, all mainline Protestant Churches in 1976 lost members except one, and the single exception was primarily due to improved methods of data collection.

To quote George Gallup again, "Evidence is mounting that the U.S. may be in an early stage of a profound religious revival, with the evangelical movement providing a powerful thrust."[3] Various factors enter into the definition of "evangelical," including a conviction of religious experience, a high respect for the Bible, and an active concern for the conversion of others.

Dean M. Kelley, who authored the provocative *Why Conserva tive Churches Are Growing*, provides some insights. "The denominations which grow are, by and large, those which do a better job at the essential function of religion, which I characterized as 'making life meaningful in ultimate terms.' " He attaches the words "strict" and "serious" to those Churches categorized as conservative or evangelical. If witnessing by example is as important as some of my respondents have stated, then Kelley's additional observation is pertinent. He says that "the most revealing data about religious behavior [is found] in actions that cost something in money, time, effort, anguish, involvement, or sacrifice. It simply *costs* more to be an Adventist than an Episcopalian. . . . in the double tithe, the time spent, the efforts made, the witnessing overtures to non-members, the constant preoccupation with the Faith, the average Adventist so far outshines the average Episcopalian that they are not even in the same category of magnitude."[4]

One church leader I interviewed contrasted the church community with Alcoholics Anonymous:

3. *Religion in America*, p. 114.
4. Dean M. Kelley, unpublished manuscript. Quoted with permission.

I'm always impressed with the way AA people treat each other. I don't want to glorify it, but I see there a certain humility and honesty that often is lacking in the Church. To be sure, they argue and fight and get angry, but they seem to be able to express it, and more freely than we can, and to be sorry, and to really love each other. I think it's always because they know their roots. They have so much in common that differences can be worked out.

The analogy fits the evangelical church people at their best because their outspoken testimony, the simplicity of the Faith, the grappling with sin and forgiveness and salvation are a reminder of common roots. When all systems are working well, such a fellowship nourishes itself and invites others to the board.

Yet did not each of the mainline Churches also begin with close fellowship? Did they not raise voices of protest against the laxity of the Church and the world of their day, huddling close against the outer darkness, cherishing the light that each member brought to the common meeting? Many of the Churches now called "mainline" were anything but that in the days of their youth. The MSU professor pointed out, "These Churches attained their size through evangelizing the frontier, all the great revivals and so forth. Lutherans came over pretty much in ethnic groups; Catholics didn't do an awful lot of evangelizing. And it doesn't seem to me that we Methodists and Presbyterians and UCC are ready to be serious about that again."

But what if the ashes were stirred up? Could the fire flare again? I think we can learn from the evangelicals. Their religion is sometimes called the "non-thinking man's" religion, and the charge has enough truth to sting. The mainline Churches do have a treasury of thought and tradition from which the evangelicals could benefit. But today evangelicals may be in the teacher's chair, pointing out what touches people deeply and changes their lives by instilling in them a new religious awareness. In so many ways— not the least of them ministry to youth—the mainline Churches have much to learn.

THE CONGREGATION'S RESPONSE

At least four forms of evangelism emerge from this study: witness by example; verbal testimony; invitations to the Church and its activities; and congregational outreach programs.

As Chapter 6 shows, many people of different Churches preferred to witness by setting a Christian example. In his book, *Power and Praise*, Merlin R. Carothers treats this approach:

Others are drawn to Christ when we praise God. If we grumble and complain as bitterly as our non-Christian friends over the many little upsetting incidents of our days, others conclude that our faith does no more for us than having no faith does for them. Unless they can see in the nitty-gritty of our daily lives that Christ makes a difference, how can we expect them to believe when we say they need Jesus?

It isn't what we say, but what we are and what we do that draws others to the Christ-life in us. Nowhere is this more apparent than in our daily lives. How do we react to delays and difficulties on the job, in emergencies, in everyday encounters? Do we react in such a way that no one sees anything different about us? Or does our reaction cause them to stop and say, "Something is different about that person. He's got something I need."[5]

A layman from Monmouth, Oregon agreed. "To me, when you become the property of Jesus Christ, you can't help but live in some way in evangelism. That may not be a tambourine and a horn on a street corner. But it is a way of living—joy, love, peace and the satisfaction in your life. Not that you're on a continual emotional high, but the way you relate to people. It's kind of like garlic on a roast . . . by George, there's some garlic there." One Mainer said with simplicity, "I think your life shows more than your mouth." An effective evangelism thrust may consist simply in reminding the congregation of this truth and exhorting them to "be what you are—the property of Jesus Christ."

Yet there is another channel for the energy and enthusiasm of a congregation: organized programs of evangelism. While

5. Merlin R. Carothers, *Power in Praise* (Plainfield, N.J.: Logos International, 1972), p. 117, Quoted with permission.

some Churches eschew door-to-door visitation, others have found that it bears fruit. The pastor of a Sarasota Christian church recalled that his 2,000 visits drew responses from only three or four families. The Lutheran Church in Holt, Michigan, on the other hand, claimed great blessings from its high-powered evangelism effort. A Japanese Free Methodist congregation in Anaheim, California went through the telephone directory to identify every person with a Japanese-sounding name, only to find themselves visiting not only Japanese Protestants, but Italian Catholics and Lebanese Moslems as well. Word of mouth, person-to-person contacts proved more effective for this ethnic community.

An outstanding Baptist layman from Dallas, Oregon warned against making the wrong kind of calls on strangers. "Most of the time people feel you're doing this because somebody told you to, or you're doing this because you feel you ought to. You're not doing this because you care. If you say to someone you know, 'You're my friend and I care and I want to share,' that's what cuts the ice. But strangers might get the feeling that you're interfering with their life or asking questions that are too personal."

Are there those whom only a close, friendly relationship will open to new possibilities, who will not change their religious stance in response to a stranger's knock on the door? Probably. There are also people who have no Christian friends, and the "cold-turkey" visit may be the Church's only means of entry into their lives. Such visits, made in conjunction with an organized evangelism program, have worked with some. People have allowed patient, serious strangers to share Christian faith with them. God's Spirit has chosen to work through these human messengers, as shown by the evidence of changed lives.

MAGNET CHURCHES

Sometimes a certain religious chemistry is at work, even in counties where the majority of the people are not affiliated with a Church. Suddenly a congregation which began on a shoestring surges with new growth and enthusiasm. And churches which had scraped along in dreary fashion, making little impact upon their communities, transform themselves into busy congregations, changing people within the fellowship as markedly as they change those unchurched men and women they draw in. In the course of visiting many congregations, I have identified four characteristics that, in different combinations, mark what I call a "magnet church":

WORSHIP, the experience on Sunday morning that makes God real;

A MINISTER who attracts, emboldens, uplifts, and communicates God's love;

PEOPLE who by their warm welcome and their confidence in the worth of their congregation, convey its benefits to outsiders; and

PROGRAMS which build up and reach out.

Concerning the worship experience, a Lutheran judicatory leader said, "Somehow I get the feeling that worship is a thing to be ground out, not necessarily a celebration. Unless the celebration experience goes through the leader of worship, it doesn't get out to the people. I can see why people drop away. It really doesn't take hold of them. I have no problems with the liturgy, but I have a problem with a leader who seems to accept it as a routine to go through without really understanding what it's all about."

The evangelical Churches, with their free and spontaneous worship forms, were often credited with making God real for people. They offer an option to that teen-ager who left a liturgical Church saying, "I feel like I'm dying, sitting there." A former Catholic says that when she moved to Belfast, Maine she felt no attraction to either the Catholic or the mainline Protestant Churches. When she first visited the Pentecostal Church in Searsport with her five children, she found that "the music is snappy and I like that, and the hand-clapping. And that's a good feeling, and you're joining in with other people who are feeling the same. And my five kids—mine are a little more lively than others—like it too. . . . I believe that teen-agers are going to bring about a transition because they are finding and expressing their own emotions in church."

Another Maine couple who joined the Searsport Full Gospel Church also found that their children really wanted to go to church once they began attending this congregation. The oldest son said, concerning his former church, "I'd like to go up there and sing, 'God's not dead.'" His mother commented, "Because they were so stiff and cold and he just didn't like that. And that's really what brought us to the new church—the fact that you could feel God and you knew that He was alive." Remarkably, in this New England county, the Full Gospel Church was alone in reporting a sizeable increase in membership and attendance. It is a magnet church. The Nazarene congregation and a few smaller churches reported limited growth, while the mainline Churches were hard put to identify previously unchurched members for me. Several could find none at all.

If some of the previosly unchurched people are immediately at home in a free, non-liturgical worship atmosphere, others appreciate a more formal approach. When she considered which Church to join, May decided on the Catholic Church in East Lansing, where she found the "mystery" she felt she needed. Dora, a member of another Catholic parish, came from a Protestant background. She remarked, "I love being Catholic—it's a whole new dimension. Just for the Sacraments, the sense of worship that's in [the] Catholic Church. I love Baptists, and they really preach the Word, but the ceremony, the Sacraments, and the worship in [the] Catholic Church—its a real personal kind of thing for me. I really experience the Lord a lot." She went on to describe her response to the Eucharist as "just the experience of Jesus."

Kathryn spoke with equal fervor about her decision to reaffiliate with the Episcopal Church. She loves the great cathedrals, religious poetry, and church music:

> I thought, "Wow! All these centuries." It's kind of neat that the cathedral has been kept and I can still see it. Of course the Episcopal Church has absolutely gorgeous music. You can't forget it, and if you grew up with it, to leave it is a terrible thing. It's not rational. It's an artistic, fairly unconscious thing, and one of the things that disturbs me about the Episcopal Church, it being a liturgical Church, is that it's so ... rational most of the time and that's a great mistake.

But where I hear that music, I think, "Oh, don't rock the tradition."

There is also a group of people who appreciate the unique strengths of mainline worship. A Presbyterian said, "That congregation appeals to me because we worship God through the spirit, but through the mind too. Its church government and the way it makes decisions is my kind of process. Not that I couldn't be comfortable in some other kinds of Churches—but that process fits me."

I found *magnet pastors* in surprisingly varied places. Of course the great congregations of Orange County point with understandable pride to the exceptional men who lead them. But I also encountered pastors elsewhere whose reputation in the congregation and community was extraordinarily high. What marks did these clergy exhibit that enabled them, like magnets, to attract and hold the loyalty and affection of large numbers of people?

Said a professional athlete in California concerning the pastor of the church he had recently joined, "Everybody told me about him and the type of individual he was." Another previously unchurched Californian, a new Lutheran, said of the change in his religious stance, "I felt like it was time for a turn in my life back to something that I felt comfortable in. And the pastor spoke on a level which I could understand." It was a feeling expressed about this particular clergyman.

A 35-year-old divorced teacher described her Presbyterian pastor and the wide influence he has had. "I know he has been in the places he has spoken to and about and for; and even if I have not been there, I can identify with him and he with me. It's very personal. Very good with words, he's a poet. He brings to the surface so much that needs to be taken care of during the week and not just on Sundays. People need that touch. He's very much loved."

When asked for the secret of Calvary Chapel, one young person answered, "One thing Chuck [Smith] has taught all the years I've been here is—get into the word of God. It's that continual giving the glory to Jesus and uplifting Him." Pastor Smith supplements relatively low-key preaching by leading Bible study and encouraging personal application. Devoid of pulpit fireworks, he invites his huge audience to read along in their own Bibles and hear Jesus' words for themselves.

Few people ascribed extraordinary preaching skills to their pastors. But magnet clergy were judged to be full of love and personal concern. They know the flock by name and show that they care. Often they put themselves on the line, as Rod said of the Catholic priest in East Lansing who helped him return to his Church:

> I got to know him as a result of hearing his Mass a couple of times and meeting him on the bridge over on campus as he was handing out the little paperbound new Bible, the *Good News*. Here was a priest who was taking his time on campus and really putting his guts out on the line and saying, "I believe in this, do you believe in it?" I imagine he got a lot of negative responses and a lot of people laughing and so forth. But he had guts enough to do it. That really caught my attention.

In answer to the question, "What is the main thing that led you to the Church?" Rod immediately said:

> Probably the individual, Father F, as a man and as a preacher. Just had that positive thing that I was really looking for, spirituality. It's not his personality, it's his spirituality—his belief and his commitment to it. I imitate him. I find myself imitating his style, because I like it. . . . He broke the traditional thing that I knew about and said, "Here's a place where you can live, and you can take this into your everyday life." That's what I was looking for in a church organization.

A third ingredient in the magnet church is the *caring membership*. One person described the congregation's attitude toward him as one of "gentle concern." Of a Catholic charismatic group she joined, Dora said, "I think that it would be the love and the sincerity and the joy that I saw in other people that brought me to the Church. The first time I went to a prayer meeting I saw people hugging each other, just sharing, just loving each other, and I was so struck by that. And after going for just a few times,

I knew they're really sincere about it. That's what attracted me more than anything else. And they were happy. So am I, now."

Jackie joined the Lutheran Church in Laguna Hills, California because of the unusually friendly reception she received when she went for the first time with her family. She said, "Usually if you go into a church no one speaks to you. If they do it's 'Oh, good morning,' and they're on their way. And you get absolutely nothing out of them, and that doesn't help. I don't care how friendly the pastor is, if the congregation turns you off, you might as well forget it." But an active "coffee group" invited the new family to join them. "They invite all the new people usually to come over and have coffee with them. And everyone comes up: 'Oh, hi! We're glad to see you, hope you come back.' And they really mean it. They were just a fantastic bunch of people. And that's why we really joined the Church."

Initiatives cited as helpful to evangelism include visiting on Sunday afternoon each person who was a new worshiper that morning; designating a greeter who introduces himself or herself to new people as they come in, writes down the name and then "presents the newcomers" to the pastor as part of the parish announcements; and giving name tags and other tokens to visitors so that the established members can easily identify them. On the other side, Lyle Schaller, in *Assimilating New Members*, points out some practices which, while not intended to be exclusionary, have the effect of blocking church expansion. He also warns congregations of the "price of growth"; the addition of new people may disrupt the status quo and force the church to move in new directions.[6]

A Presbyterian pastor in Orange County said:

We're trying to develop our inner strengths, inner life of fellowship, nurturing each other, then from that point on let it extend into the community. This church would represent a kind of extended family. I think the church has to intentionally look at itself more peculiarly in that light, and not

6. Lyle Schaller, *Assimilating New Members* (Nashville: Abingdon, 1975), pp. 69 ff. and 124 ff.

just [be] a place where people come together and get band-aids. That individuals feel that they're nourished for another week, and during the week we're not only thinking about what the pastor said, but we're thinking about someone else in that congregation's concern. To be conscious of your brother and his needs and loving him unconditionally is what grace is all about. It's a real source of power.

Finally, magnet churches have *outstanding programs*. These programs meet needs, reach out into the community and convey in some way the principal values of the congregation. The first contacts that some interviewees reported with a specific congregation came through a counseling service, a Boy Scout troop, a crisis hotline, a visiting choir, a meditation course, and a Bible study group, to give just a few examples. A southern California pastor noted, "We have an awful lot of people that have talked about this church to neighbors, to friends; we've kind of spread like fire through a local youth football program here in a way that's incredible. We've started to get coaches and assistant coaches and what have you, and families are getting involved in Confirmation." Kirk, a member of a Lansing Christian Reformed church, described a youth program of sports, art, crafts, and camping where he as youth leader is "going to get these kids there and then we're going to show them that I'm not such a bad guy."

Seven o'clock on a weekday morning might not be thought a good time for formal church services, but some have found a congregational breakfast at that hour an opportunity for close fellowship and sharing. One respondent called his congregation's breakfast, which attracts 10 to 15 people each week, "mind challenging":

It makes you think why you are a Christian and it's primarily for laypeople, lay ministers, if we may call outselves that, that do want to introduce their feelings to other people. I find it difficult in talking to people at work to discuss religious matters. This morning group has helped. Cook a little breakfast and sit around and talk and exercise one another's thoughts on what you have done to openly discuss with someone else your faith. And relate back and forth as to what other people have done or what other people felt. And how you finally decide that once in a while you can just turn it all over to God. That it will be done, that you don't have to worry about it quite as much as you thought you did.

In Costa Mesa, California the large, independent Calvary Chapel offers a weekly breakfast that draws over 200 men. The clergy are barely visible. In fact, there seems to be no leadership at all—many participate, offer prayers, lead in singing.

Programs are aimed at youth, singles, divorced people, the aged, business people, the troubled, the cultured, sophisticated seekers and sports enthusiasts. Targeting—identifying needs and striving to meet them—may be the key to becoming a magnet church using a programmatic approach.

PROBLEMS TO WORK ON

How would we rate our church if we were outsiders? One newspaper's religion editor is said to visit churches and assign them a rating. Like a food editor visiting restaurants, he checks the important things that a newcomer would notice. We could all spend a profitable church council meeting evaluating our image, our worship, our music, our friendliness and so on, as if we were people just dropping in.

Briefly, here are some problems the people I interviewed identified that may be relevant to such an evaluation. As far as Catholics are concerned:

Sermons are not very stirring. One person commented that the pastor would be more effective if he would just share his own personal faith and hope in God and relate that faith to everyday life.

Priests often do not seem to know their people, perhaps because parishes are too large. This lack of contact was seen by some as a reason for dropping out and not returning.

An impersonal quality can also mark the parish as a whole. Large congregations sometimes strike the visitor as cold and disinterested—anything but communities. Alienation, a curse of modern living, should not be the accepted mode of congregational life.

As far as Protestants are concerned:

The preacher is so prominent in worship that if he fails, there is almost nothing else to vitalize the worship service. The word of Christ must be effectively preached; otherwise the service loses much of its value.

Churches cannot simply be verbal institutions with low-key music and a lot of talk, talk, talk. Contrast the typical Protestant service with a charismatic prayer experience. Without the emphasis on meeting Christ in communion, or the outpouring of *ex corde* prayer, or the honest sharing of testimony, people's emotions may never be touched.

A sense of spirituality is lacking when the service becomes too much of a lecture and the people sit passively agreeing or disagreeing. The practice of meditation and prayer is a good corrective. The goal is to experience Christ, not to understand him.

Finally, both Catholics and Protestants could benefit from a conviction that what is happening in church is valuable, helpful, and beautiful, and so important that they are willing to show "gentle concern" and to speak a word of hope or invitation to those outside the Church's fellowship.

HOPE FOR THE FUTURE

Many respondents from different corners of the country who are new church members said "the answers aren't showing up anywhere else." It is a word of challenge to the Church to keep finding those answers. According to the Gallup study of the unchurched, many people affirm Christian principles, at least in the abstract. This may indicate a readiness to listen, to try, to give the Church another chance. How many of these unchurched men and women have put their faith in a bureau drawer, ready to be used when needed? Some people are looking into a bleak future and saying that it will be needed—soon. A Church that is confident of its message and its worth can speak out at a time when "the answers aren't showing up anywhere else."

In a recent book on the Church and singles, *Saturday Night, Sunday Morning*, Lutheran pastor Nick Christoff offers the denominations a challenge. "The Church has the means and the power to become the healer of the multitude of problems it has been accused of creating. The message of Christ calls for love of God and of one another, compassion, kindness, humility, gentleness, and patience. This was the message in the beginning, and it remains our most cherished goal to the end. Why have we let ourselves grow so indifferent to one another? What can be done to shorten the distances between us?"[7]

Those who were outside the Church for so long may help us to see our strengths and weaknesses from a new perspective. Have their voices been heard within the administrative structures of the Church? Has their new appreciation of the Church been voiced in congregational councils and committees? They may have enthusiasm that will light fires—if they get a chance. A pastor in California said that change occured when the officers of the congregation, who had been in their positions for years, were gradually replaced by a new breed. Christoff suggests that each congregation insist that singles be given access to positions of leadership, that the Church's lay ministry not be restricted to members of nuclear families. And what of the unique contributions of youth, women, the aged, artists, and every other bearer of gifts? The problems, challenges, and strengths of a church may look different to those who have only recently joined. They can add their perspective, contributing to the enrichment of the whole congregation.

Douglas Johnson, a religious researcher and consultant, writes, "It is likely that a turnaround has been reached in membership. Gains by some of the mainline denominations can be expected within the next few years, and a mood of growth will replace apprehension about continued decline. The reasons for the likely increase are the focus upon a clear purpose for the religious body, emphasis upon evangelism and education, and changes in the population, including aging and birth rates."[8] In this cau-

7. Nick Christoff, *Saturday Night, Sunday Morning* (San Francisco: Harper & Row, 1978), pp. 107-108. Quoted with permission.
8. *Religion in America*, p. 109. Quoted with permission.

tiously optimistic prediction, I would highlight the "focus upon a clear purpose for the religious body." Before we can do anything we have to know what we are about and why. We have to count the cost and talk sacrifice. Those who take their own destinies seriously will listen.

Appendix

Questions for Congregational Study

Members of a congregation might find it helpful to consider questions raised by formerly unchurched people, and to apply them to their own situation. The following questions, drawn from the interviews recorded in the preceding pages, are offered as a start:

1. Many people who visit our church have overcome great obstacles in order to enter our doors for the first time. How can we assure them that they are indeed welcome?
2. Are our members happy about being part of our congregation? If they are, why don't they tell others? If they are not, how can we search for solutions to the problems?
3. Do we provide any less formal occasions when people who are not "congenital church members" might feel more at ease in visiting our church?
4. Why do people who talk easily about other subjects become silent when the opportunity arises to talk about religion?
5. One person interviewed complained that no one showed concern when she was "falling away." How do we reach out to those showing signs of slipping out through the back door of our church?
6. What programs might open up the congregation to new experiences of nurture for members? Spiritual retreats, athletics, religious drama, church breakfasts, for example, seemed important for some.
7. How available is our church and its staff? Does the church secretary, as initial contact in many instances, help or hinder people when they call? Are there ways for the church to be open apart from services?

8. What are our strengths as a congregation? What do we have to offer the unchurched? Why would anyone want to join our church? How can we make our invitation better known?

9. Spiritual journeys for many include a period of youthful wandering from the Church. What does this tell us about parish education? pastoral care? program priorities?

10. Can we identify with any of the interviewees? Why? In what way does our spiritual experience compare with theirs?

Typescripts of several full-length interviews are available for personal or group study. Inquiries may be addressed to the author, at the Lutheran Council in the U.S.A., 360 Park Avenue South, New York, N.Y. 10010.